The Peover Eye

Fishing along a Cheshire River

John Lea

illustrations by G. Ashley Hunter

To Celia who made it all possible

Two dreams entwined
Two paths, one road
Two hearts, one mind
Two lives, one soul

When the Good Lord adds up your appointed days, he doesn't count any days spent fishing..

Anon.

Number ....
of a limited edition of 975

CHURNET VALLEY BOOKS
1 King Street, Leek. ST13 5NW. 01538 399033

ISBN 1904546 01 3

ST JAMES CHURCH
GAWSWORTH

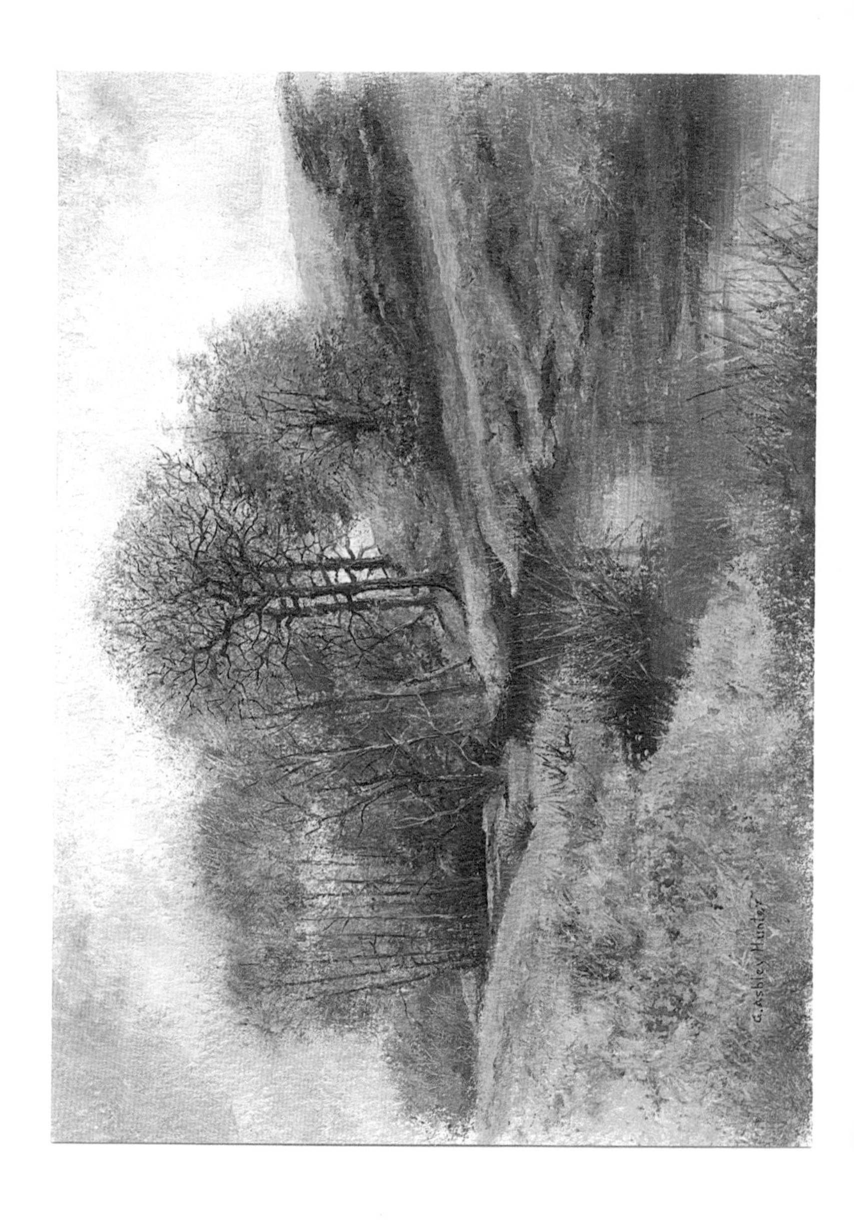
G. Ashley Hunter

One
THE RIVER

When a wildlife artist and an author are privileged to wander the beautiful but secluded banks of a small Cheshire river for many years, what could the outcome be? It has to be a book, not just about trout fishing, but all about the wildlife sharing that haven.

I share the fishing rights on the Peover Eye with the Artist G. Ashley Hunter (Bill to his friends) and another friend, Gerald Stevens. Although the story is mainly a record of my days by the water the artwork comes from Bill's own experiences.

Frequently, along the riverbanks, we meet the hunting fox, the perky little wren and the dazzling Kingfisher. We may even catch the odd trout to make our experience complete. Although I try to explain which fly we use, when and why, don't expect an expert fishing treatise.

For most of its length the Peover Eye meanders through trees and meadows, out of sight of both public and fishermen alike. On our length, steep heavily wooded banks provide just the right habitat to make it so alive with wildlife. No house or road overlooks us or is even near.

So join us for a few hours on the banks of this peaceful little river, which flows through a beautiful

Bill's cartoon skills

yet mainly forgotten part of Cheshire. *"You can have the fishing. Bring a couple of friends in with you to share the cost if you want, but I don't want a crowd".* That agreement by a Cheshire Farmer was the start to one of the most pleasurable experiences of my life. He added one condition - he, his family and his friends could fish when they liked and with whatever method they liked. No fly fishing only rules!

For me it was a dream comes true. Not just that I could fish, but that the fishing was so quiet and undisturbed. Lower down, the Peover Eye runs through open and fairly flat meadows. Along this upper length it cuts through a steep sided valley, which I presume was gouged out by a glacier in the long distant ice age. The result of that primeval force

Bill's cartoon skills

is that the bottom of that valley, once the bed of that ice age river, is now a fairly flat narrow strip through which the brook winds and meanders back and fro, as if trying to escape. In the season, along the banks a few clusters of small wild daffodils dance in the spring breeze, and occasional clumps of primroses catch the eye.

To get the best out of fishing it needs to be shared, not that I need someone by my side all the time. It's nice though to have friends involved and - dare I say - to help share the cost. My two companions chose themselves really. I've both fished and shot with Gerald Stevens for more than thirty years. Although I haven't known Bill (G. Ashley Hunter) for quite that length of time he shares my countryside interests and, as a professional artist, can capture them on canvas.

We have sat together by a pond in a cold east wind waiting for 'flighting' duck. Bill even sent me a personalised Christmas card reminding me of one such evening, so cold that when the duck finally came our fingers were too numb to pull the trigger. Then in summer with fly rod in hand we have laughed together about the one that got away. It's a good test of friendship when, after four or five hours in someone's company, you've failed to catch an over shy trout or perhaps to shoot a marauding fox, and yet still feel completely relaxed together. Such is the true field sport friendship.

As a young man Bill worked on farms in both Gawsworth and elsewhere in Cheshire before running his own small pig and poultry farm. Working with livestock provided ready subjects for his natural artistic skill, and now as a professional artist he is able to depict nature as it is in the wild. This book is as much his experiences as mine, for Bill is a natural observer who seldom fishes without a camera in his bag. One can sit relaxed to paint a scene, but with wildlife, things happen so fast. Bill and his camera are often in action to capture that fleeting moment.

Bill's enjoyment of nature has been there from a boy. He says that when he was at school he often got into trouble for looking out of the window.

He is still the same now - nature holds such a fascination for him that he is easily lured from the studio to the riverbank.

Having now lost the urge to shoot Bill is happy just watching all nature. His countryman's sense of humour is captured in his farming cartoons, which are enjoyed by many. For these he uses the signature ASH, perhaps he thinks the serious artist and the cartoonist shouldn't mix. Many of you have seen his cartoons in Down the Cobbled Stones and in Reach for My Countryside, and in this book he will be revealing more of his impish humour.

We often go to the water on our own; perhaps sometimes our fly-casting is better not witnessed! On the occasions when we are there together we usually wander in different directions to fish, only meeting two or three times through an evening. It's this complete quietness coupled with a capacity to just sit and watch that has provided the material for the book.

The river, well perhaps it is only a brook really, is no clear chalk stream meandering across open meadows. Instead its heavily tree-lined earth banks give a dark and murky colour to the water. As the stream gurgles and zigzags on its timeless way, the heavy rains of each new winter reshape it, and in the resulting deep holes, perhaps hiding in the roots of the prolific alder, or behind the stumps of large oak, trout grow large and fat.

In one such spot, swelled by heavy winter rain, the current had swirled into the opposite bank by a large oak tree to form a deep swirling eddy, which through the summer months became just a small quiet pool. The barbed wire fence, which had previously followed the bank side, was still nailed to the oak tree and now stretched across the newly formed pool. When I noticed a sizable trout had taken up residence there, I tried to cast across to him. Although he continued to feed greedily under the barbed wire he couldn't be tempted out. Of course I tried to drop my fly a little closer and a little closer until - well you can guess what happened. I returned some days later to find a second fly hanging from the barbed wire alongside mine. A couple or more weeks went past, and by now the wire was getting crowded, before Bill joined me for an evening of confession.

It was perhaps a week later when Gerald drove me down to the brook. We went our different ways along the banks as usual. When we met later in the evening the conversation went like this:

Me. "Did you see all those flies hanging on that wire?"

"What wire? Where?"

A lengthy explanation from me.

"You mean just past that big oak? I took a nice trout there, but I didn't notice any flies."

There must be a Chinese proverb that goes,

'Man who hookee flies on wire catchee no fish.'

Behind the lovely old black and white hall in Gawsworth, springs rise from the ground to create Gandysbrook. The overflow from the spring fed fishponds in front of both the Hall and the church also run into the same brook. More springs, rising just to the east of Gawsworth village, form Benbrook, which in turn joins Gandysbrook to the west of the village. I think of both brooks as the source of the Peover Eye.

St James Church
Gawsworth

After joining together, just above the now derelict site of the old Gawsworth watermill, the brook changes its name. Snapebrook then flows through Siddington, picking up Fanshaw brook on its way down toward the Cheshire Plane. Met in Chelford by another large tributary from Astle and Birtles, the two brooks create the Peover Eye. Called the "Pevr Ee" in Anglo-Saxon times, it would have been an important waterway, used for both transport and trade across mid Cheshire.

The Eye flows through Over Peover and Lower Peover and a few other Peovers. Although I can think of Peover Superior, Peover Inferior, Peover Heath and Nether Peover, I am not sure that even that list is complete, but we, who live near by, just lump them together as either Lower Peover or Over Peover. Running on through Plumley there is still an outline of prolific alders but the brook is no longer in a steep sided valley. Finally through Wincham, after struggling through a chemical works, the Peover Eye joins the River Weaver at Winnington near to Northwich.

We are all connected with this very Cheshire river in one-way or other. Bill's home and studio are on the Henbury side of Macclesfield, within the brooks catchment's area. Gerald was brought up close to the old water mill in Gawsworth, which by then had ceased to work. Although in recent years the mill pool has been renovated, Gerald's memory of it was of no more than a rushy hollow. As a boy he fished the upper reaches of the Peover Eye, as well as nearby ponds and lakes. The rolling banks of the quiet Gawsworth farmland provided plenty of wildlife interest for Gerald and his four brothers.

I now live in Gawsworth, but my first link with the brook was much lower down stream. The farm where I was born lay on the banks of the Eye in Nether Peover. I wrote in detail about that time in *Down the Cobbled Stones*, how, through the farming depression in the 1930s my Father helped to feed his young family by using a nightline to catch big trout. In those days the brook was a noted trout stream, with much of its length reserved for the gentry. My older brothers remember leaning over a bridge on the way to school, to watch clouds of mayfly dancing above the water.

Mother's father was a fisherman, who, living on the edge of Lower Peover in the late 19th century, would no doubt fish in this brook. Alas, because he died before Mother married, I have no memory of him, other than that as children we used to play with his violin and melodeon. We also committed the sin of sins by using his old greenheart fly rod to worm fish for little perch.

In those days brown trout bred prolifically in the brook. They were so numerous that when my Father and his younger brothers were invited to fish the length covered by this book, just before the 1918 war, my Uncle Joe caught seventeen trout in one evening, though not fly-fishing - in that age, most fly fishermen carried a tin of worms for 'quiet periods'.

When my family moved from Nether Peover to Toft, the closest school for me to attend was still Lower Peover. During my first few months of schooling, Mother walked with me to school, pushing her bicycle alongside. Then, after pedalling home to run a large farmhouse, Mum later returned to walk home with me in the afternoon.

Going the back way into school, down Barrow Brow to cross the little bridge over the Eye onto Church Walk, I can remember stopping to stare into the rippling water, but Mum would hurry me on through the graveyard, via the lichgate, and onto the cobbled stones by the school. If you step through there today that scene has barely changed since the school was first opened in 1710, except that now children are ferried back and to by car.

With the brook rippling alongside the graveyard, Lower Peover church remains very much as it has for over seven hundred years. St Oswald's justifiably claims to be one of the most beautiful black and white churches in England. Nestling next to the graveyard, the Bells of Peover pub gives a timeless and romantic feeling to the village. I have described this lovely hamlet in some detail because it is the only one that lies close to the brook, and one of the few places where cottage gardens run down to the water's edge.

Over Peover also has its old church and a much more stately hall - its claim to fame is that General Patten was billeted there in the middle years of the last War. The Peover Eye does not run through the middle of Over Peover village, as it does through Lower Peover, so Over Peover residents are often unaware of their beautiful river. Many of them are recent incomers, who live in extended and luxurious homes well away from this hidden picturesque valley. The church is well worth a visit and there are three pubs in the Parish, each serving good food - perhaps The Dog has claim to most awards for its culinary excellence. We always knew it as the 'Gay Dog', but the word now has different connotations, so it is just The Dog again.

There were at least nine watermills on the Eye or its tributaries, and members of the Lea family at one time or other have run both Lower and Over Peover watermills. Further up stream, on the border of Over Peover and Lower Withington, are the more complete remains of another water mill known as Bate Mill. In it is an original flush toilet, in fact a double seat where you could companionably sit side by side - right over the raging mill tailrace - that has to be a flush toilet with a difference.

2
MARCH

March can be a month of wind and rain; even so, on the first reasonable day, we try to get down to the water to assess the damage of winter. With no rocks to protect the banks, floods can have a dramatic effect in this type of stream. This one suffers more than some because of the run off from the large sand quarries up stream. Now that Lapwing Lane has been closed to allow the two largest quarries to join together, the result is, what is said to be the largest man-made hole in Europe. Such is its size that it needs a three-mile long conveyer belt to carry the excavated sand across the quarry.

Most of the sand produced is very fine silica, which has many uses in industry, including glass making. But silica sand needs washing, which of course produces a lot of dirty water. Before controls were put in place, much of that dirty water came down the brook, both from the cleaning process and from the quarry face. Nowadays all that waste water has to be caught in vast lagoons where the sediment can settle. This is not such an expense to the quarry because some of the settled dirty sand is used in industries, such as in plastic production.

Creation of such quarries is not completely

damaging to nature. Now, as we fish in spring, we often hear the piping call of oystercatchers flying overhead. They now breed on the sandy banks around the quarries, and sometimes out on nearby fields, where they nest on the bare soil in amongst the potato drills. Little ringed plovers have also made use of this change of habitat, and sand martins colonise a sand face each year, digging nest holes in the near vertical sand cliff. The quarry deliberately works elsewhere until the sand martins' breeding season is over.

Where the dirty water flows back into the settling lagoons, the resulting shallow shelf of waste sand attracts large numbers of wading birds and other water birds. Each autumn, a few hundred Lapwings (peewits to we Cheshire farmers) also congregate there. In fact if you travel up Lapwing Lane from the Chelford end, at the point where the road now ends, the mixed flock of birds paddling around the outflow can easily be seen from the right hand side of the road.

Although the water is now much cleaner there is still a lot of fine soft sand swilling about in the stream. Branches or trees lodged across the brook can create new pools, or more usually, sand banks, where old pools have been. One sad result is that the trout have not bred naturally here for about fifty years. Trout spawn in the gravel along the shallow fast flowing runs of a stream, but in our river, fine sand drifts over the newly laid trouts' eggs and smothers them. I can only presume the sand must also affect the aquatic insects, because May fly are increasing as the brook has become cleaner.

When I was writing *Down the Cobbled Stones,* I got a bit excited after finding some small brown trout in the water. I wrote how I thought they were the first hatched in the stream for many years. Alas not so; I discovered later that the Prince Albert Fishing Club had introduced some brown trout fry in the lower length of the river they fish.

Each spring we need one or two visits to remove debris, bough a few trees, and trim intruding roots. To Gerald and myself, it's just more work, but Bill enjoys it immensely. Perhaps the winter in his studio, with delicate brush and easel, leaves him with surplus energy? With waders on, and saw or axe in hand, he attacks any offending branch, either in or out of the water, with great relish and enthusiasm

On one occasion Bill was struggling in the water with a sunken tree bough and called for me to hold one end from the bank, while he waded to the other end. As we were both lifting it clear of the water, a bullhead (a small fish that some call millers' thumbs) was wriggling in a knothole. Anyway, it now gave an extra heave to splash back into the stream. Looking into that little hole, which was only about two inches in diameter by one to two inches deep, we saw some eggs. Staying there at the risk of death, that brave little fish had been protecting seven tiny eggs.

The male bullhead usually creates a nest in gravel before inviting his mate to lay her eggs, but here, in the mud, he had made do with a ready made one in the sunken timber. Had we not disturbed him he would have proudly stood guard over them until they had hatched. What a two inch long bullhead would fight needs a bit of imagination on my part. To a trout or pike, or even a dabbling mallard, that little bullhead would be a handy snack; obviously bravery is not measured by size.

It is important not to be too enthusiastic when cutting underwater roots or even cutting over-hanging branches. One year we over-cleaned one length, only to find that the fish moved to other parts, where there were roots to hide among and low branches to bask under. Trout are shy creatures, and, even when feeding, a trout often lies in wait under the shadow of a low branch or over-hanging weed, taking passing food with a quick strike or rise, then returning to their safe retreat.

Long stretches of the lower brook are so densely overgrown with alder trees that it is almost impossible to cast a fly. Wading is an option, but the bottom is soft and some of the holes are too deep even for waders. A guest with me one day, who shall be nameless, overbalanced and went into one of these holes head first. When he stood up, the water was over his thighs, and when he then bent down to feel for his lost glasses, there was little of him out of the water. To save myself from temptation I only wear walking boots - my one wet foot came from trying to retrieve a valued fly.

"LOST SOMETHING ?"

We are fortunate, in that, on the top stretch, we have about seventy yards of relatively open brook on both banks. On the next length, a fairly flat meadow follows one bank side, which being mostly free of trees allows us to fish with relative ease. This narrow strip of grassland, perhaps at its widest no more than fifty yards, is enclosed by an equally high tree covered steep bank on the other side of the river, which curves back to the brook side at each end. As we fish from the meadowside, the opposite bank rises almost vertical from the water's edge, perhaps some fifty feet or more in height, and heavily wooded with a mixture of alder, hawthorn and oak. One would need to be a mountain goat to fish this bank.

One of our first concerns each spring is the whereabouts of the kingfishers. They still breed along the Peover Eye, even on the smaller streams, all the way up into Gawsworth, and we happily share our fishing with them throughout the year. Each pair claim about a mile of brook, and now, in early spring, they are protecting their boundaries from intrusion by other kingfishers. Both sexes seem to do this - but I presume the male has the added problem of protecting his wife's honour from every good-looking suitor that happens by.

When we hear a high-pitched piping whistle we look up, just in time to see a flash of brilliant colour sweeping under branches, just above the water line. I say 'we' look up, because I have noticed that both Bill and Gerald stop work immediately at the sound of one. They even stop fishing - which shows the hold this colourful little bird has on each of us.

Kingfishers usually nest in a steep bank next to running water. Although I have heard of nests in woodland banks well away from water, I have not actually seen one. Usually they nest where the winter floods have eroded the bank causing a landslide that in turn has left an almost vertical face of bare sand. They dig a long horizontal burrow, some two feet into the sand face. To confuse you there can be some false holes, or perhaps old ones left from the year before; whichever, it makes finding the real nest very difficult.

There is only one rule in our little club - we should enjoy our fishing. By convention we keep the more open length for fly-fishing, but on the lower length among the trees we have no inhibitions about casting a worm - usually when the water is high in early or late season, or when the grand-children come to fish. Both Gerald and Bill's grand-children have caught their first trout here, but mine are still a bit too young.

Although a warm late March day can encourage trout to move, I will explain which flies we use in April, because usually the water is just too high and fast flowing in March to get pleasure from casting a fly. Once the season is open, I look for a nice afternoon to take a short rod and a few worms down among the alders on the lower length.

This may seem a strange way to start a book that's mainly about fly-fishing, so let me explain a little. Each spring I enjoy this wander along the banks, it renews my bond with the lovely valley and gives me a chance to see the condition of the brook and how the trout have faired over the winter. Early in the year, trout seldom rise here under the dense alder trees, but on a warm day they can be feeding hungrily deep down among the roots. It is possible to get down to some of them with a weighted fly on a sunken line but, alas, polio in my youth has left me without the necessary agility to dodge in and out of the numerous trees. But a heavy lead shot will take a worm down to the fish for me with more ease.

When I clean trout for the table I usually have a look at the stomach contents. Looking through the entrails - like a witch doctor - can reveal a lot of information. As the season progresses, caddis larvae become the main diet of these bottom-feeding trout, but in March they seem to feed on a variety of insects. Later in the season, some trout develop such a liking for snails, they feed on little else - yet they are still good to eat. So far I have not caught one of those snail feeding trout on a fly, but it seems the humble worm appeals to all persuasions. There are nearly 200 species of sedge or caddisfly (flies with roof shaped wings) but you don't need to know much about them this early in the season, other than that in this brook our species's larvae coats itself with grit and sand and stay right near the bottom. I will come back to them and the adult caddis in a later chapter.

Wandering quietly along the bank I could see an early hatch of young mallard ducklings scuttling round a bend ahead. Being the first of the season, I knew those little chaps would be lucky to survive, because, dependant as they are on hatching insects for food, if there is nothing for a trout to rise to, there cannot be much for them.

The people who own the next length of brook to ours gave us permission to stock and fish their water. They thought it would be nice to see trout moving when they took a walk along the banks, but two years after we had put fish in, they still had not managed to see a fish rise or move. Yet on their length, where there are a few spots open enough to drop a fly in, Bill has had some enjoyable evenings floating a nymph round the trees, and with good results too, if you don't count the number of flies lost.

Brown trout in a brook have a pecking order, the biggest fish choosing to lie in the best spots, the next biggest the second best, and so on. On one March day, I caught two brownies within twenty yards of each other, both a good pound and a half. One was a longer fish than the other, perhaps it had not wintered as well, but it was still in the best pool. With two of the best pools vacant there would be a general move among the fish hierarchy on that stretch. Rainbows are different in that they wander about much more, often ending up far from where they are put in. Their restless nature must cause havoc to the feeding life of the more orderly brown trout.

With a nice brace of trout on the bank, my mind often starts to wander. This time it was a grey squirrel I saw scampering from tree to tree on the opposite bank. Then, as it leapt agilely from tree to tree, the farm's collie joined me. The dog's master also arrived, in time to watch the squirrel take a short cut, crossing a small meadow from one block of trees to the next. An alert fox, which must have been watching from the wood at the far side, cut the squirrel off in the open meadow. But the dog, who had already accounted for the odd fox in the past, saw what was happening, and he quickly swam the brook and raced round to cut the fox off.

Standing low down by the water's edge I couldn't see over the opposite bank, but because he was standing higher up the bank, my farming host gave a running commentary. Reynard is not so easily caught, he just dropped his catch in front of the dog and ran. The collie thought he had won because he gained a squirrel, which he brought proudly back to us. The fox thought he had won because he had outwitted the dog. And the squirrel; well he didn't think much about anything at all.

A tall alder tree is a good place for a pair of carrion crows to nest. One spring day I sat quietly on the bank, watching two working hard at their home building. I was surprised how far they flew for material - one of them returned from across the fields carrying a twig that looked to be about two feet long. Well it was more of a stick really, and he gripped it in the middle for good balance. I could only wonder how his mate was going to weave it into a nest. Anyway there was a considerable amount of crow argument when he landed with it. Probably crow language for *"What am I supposed to do with that thing?"*

Carrion crows are not only larger than rooks, they have many different habits. Whereas rooks nest in the same communal rookery site each year, rebuilding old nests or building new ones in the same group of trees, and all of it done in a noisy, stick stealing, argumentative frenzy, carrion crows are just the opposite, building in isolation, and going about their task in quiet secrecy, seldom using the same tree for a second year.

Carrion crows will not tolerate any other bird flying into their nesting territory. As I watched this pair even the humble wood pigeon was attacked when he landed to feed on the nearby meadow. When a large heron came near, the crows attacked immediately - I love to watch a heron ducking and weaving trying to avoid the crows' swooping dives. Perhaps I enjoy it more because of all the trout a heron stabs with his stiletto beak, leaving many to suffer with horrible wounds!

Later in the season, when a buzzard got the same treatment, he turned aggressively towards the crow, and the crow 'beat it' with a frenzied flapping of both wings and feet. After that the crows treated the buzzard with a lot more respect, keeping a safe distance with just an occasional restrained attack.

"AND JUST WHAT DO YOU THINK I CAN DO WITH THAT?"

3
APRIL

Although some ewes and lambs share our meadow, each spring in April they are moved across the farm to their summer pastures. This flock lambs early, so that, hopefully, some of the best lambs will be ready in time to catch the Easter market. After lambing inside the farm buildings, the ewes and young lambs come into this sheltered valley until they get a little stronger. Lambing inside not only protects the lambs from the severe weather it also keeps the hungry foxes a bay. Even so if too many ewes lamb at the same time, they overflow the post-lambing pens and have to be released a little earlier than desirable. It is almost impossible for mum to keep adventurous twins or triplets under control, and alas, the lurking fox takes advantage of any wayward lamb.

I can remember as a boy watching young lambs playing king of the castle. Perhaps I still haven't grown up because this April I sat for ages just watching them gambolling and playing along the brook bank side. One suddenly leapt on a tree root to defend it from all comers. He fended off one attacker from the front but a second butted him off from the rear. Then they were racing along the bank again. How can such a playful lamb grow into a dull old sheep? Is there a human similarity?

Through late March, and into April, trout are mainly feeding below the surface. When the April weather begins to warm up, more fly life comes to the water, which in turn tempts the fish to look up to see what may be landing on the surface.

On the high bank opposite the meadow, the mixture of oak trees, interspersed with hawthorn and alders, hold a lot of insects. Where they hang over the brook trout can be feeding hungrily and yet it can be difficult to identify what they are feeding on. I am not going to name one fly as more important than others this early in the season. I believe that nearly a thousand different insect species live in an oak tree and perhaps hawthorn holds the next highest number. It follows that there has to be a lot of insects that have over-wintered in them and here they are right over the brook! As they become active in Spring, some drop into the brook by accident - some with a splash that even I can copy!

The insect life on a brook is vastly different to that on still water; here the variation within yards is fantastic. Sunshine or shade, wind blown or wind break, tree cover or open water; any combination of these creates a series of microclimates where, within yards of each other, fish can be feeding on completely different insects. As the day progresses the sun moves round, which means that each length of a brook is ever changing and always fascinating.

Through the first part of the month, away from the trees on the open stretch, very few fish break the surface but of course they are feeding deeper in the water. Many kinds of nymphs spend two years in the water before emerging; a few species of mayfly take three years to reach maturity. If you imagine all the various flies that breed in a brook, then think of the number of fish, not just trout but all the course fish from bullhead to pike who feed on those nymphs and larvae every day. It is obvious that there has to be millions of insects moving around in the water.

Hungry Spring trout are not too selective and feed on a wide variety of those millions of insects in April. Even so, I watched for some time and not one trout broke the surface. I used to enjoy fishing a wet fly, but now I prefer to look for a rising trout to cast a dry fly to. It was back to the high bank and overhanging oaks on the upper length to find the early season action. Almost any black fly, wet or dry, will take these hungry fish, but I lose so

many in branches that I can end up fishing with a third or even fourth choice.

A black fly with a ginger hackle, or even a hawthorn, is worth a try. I am convinced that some individual hawthorn fly are about well before their recognised season in late April. Remember that trout will not be feeding on any one fly exclusively, so to cover a few possibilities, I often fish a white winged black fly, fishing them either dry or wet, just under the surface, and casting up stream if possible, but if not, from whichever direction I can cover a feeding fish. In fact a dry fly that becomes so water logged it sits in, rather than on the surface film, mimics a fly that has accidentally splashed down and can take these early spring fish.

Every time I fish opposite the steep bank a wren seems to be hopping about in the briars and deadnettle stalks opposite. The wrens along the brook seem to have developed a tolerance of my presence and boldly hop around quite close. Never still, they flit from stem to

stem to briar in the most boastful way, chest out, head back, a burst of song, seemingly too loud for such a tiny bird, which seems to proclaim their right to share the brook with me.

To hold trout in the open length of brook, we build about four small dams, consisting of a few large stones or pieces of concrete rolled into place. We then put smaller pieces on top to give a rise of about a foot. In fact, usually we old men stand back while one of my nephews bravely wades in. Even with youth and strength it cannot be done until the depth of water in the brook falls low enough to allow a person to stand and work in the flow. The dams must be removed again in September, before the reverse happens and the autumn rains swell the brook again. They only create small pools, but these, plus the small waterfalls from each dam, add considerably to the quality of our fly-fishing.

The reason for removing the dams is simply that sand settling in them would soon fill the pool above each dam. When the stones are removed the winter floods soon flush that sediment out and away. I also suspect there is some law against building a permanent dam on any watercourse.

When the dams were complete, a pair of grey wagtails soon claimed one of the resulting small waterfalls. Later this pair will nest in the farm buildings, but first they use the insect life on the brook to build up their body reserves after the hard winter. I am always amused to watch them catching insects. Grey wagtails seem so busy, always on the move with such a jaunty walk or hopping from stone to stone, and when they fly up to catch an insect there is such an untidy flurry of wings and tail. I can't help comparing them to the spotted flycatchers that return to my garden at home each May. The flycatchers intercept insects with such neat precision, catching them on the wing, before returning to a favoured perch - there to wait again, quiet and relaxed, for the next unlucky insect or butterfly to come by.

In late April we stock our length with a few twelve to fourteen inch brown trout. We vary the numbers to avoid over stocking and only put them in the upper fly-fishing length - fish travel down stream soon enough. For many years our suppliers were Trent Trout Fisheries, and their fish were always healthy. When I see trout on other waters with deformed fins, I wonder why people buy such fish. Fin deformity is caused by the fish being overcrowded in the hatcheries ponds, which causes them to bite each other's fins, in their feeding frenzy. The owner of Trent Trout Fisheries, Michael Leeny, always took a personal pride in the health of his fish. they were always in perfect condition, but, alas, he has now sold the business. It should not be difficult to spot the difference between new and old stock other than by size.

Before Michael's retirement, the delivery day became something of a ritual. Michael would bring out his flask and sandwiches and we would do the same. The life of the brook would then go on around us while we sat on the bank side, swapping tall fishing stories. The begging labradors also took an active part in the proceedings. I must confess that releasing a few trout seemed to take several hours.

The last year that Michael came with the fish he and Bill were releasing the last tub of fish when they saw a trout, seemingly on its side, floating back downstream towards them. When it came close they realised it was in fact held by a large pike. When the pike saw Bill it released its victim and fled. I managed to net that live trout later and its wounds were horrendous with deep gashes across both flanks. The pike in our length of brook are not numerous, some years we catch none; in others two or three; and the most caught in one year was six. If we left them to enjoy themselves they would take a lot of trout and so they must come out.

I carry a small spinning rod and plug in the boot of my car for just this sort of occasion, so I was soon in action, but although the pike was still active, the only thing to take my plug was an overhanging oak branch. With no reserve spinner I hunted through my tackle box in the car boot and found a large ugly yellow fly that came free with something or other in the distant past. It was so unreal I couldn't believe any fish would take it. Even with a wire trace I had to add a lead shot to its nose to give it sufficient weight to cast from a spinning reel. Within ten or fifteen minutes I had caught three trout and a half-pound perch but the pike refused to strike my lure even when I pulled it right past its nose.

Bill had gone with Michael to help him release fish on nearby water. He returned expecting to see a dead pike on the bank, and when it wasn't there he made a few rude comments about my fishing ability. Putting his fishing tackle together, he quickly joined in with a lure of his own. With the two of us casting at the one active pike I was sure it would have to take one or the other of our lures, but not so. We had to watch in frustration while the pike struck at the newly stocked trout in a feeding frenzy. That marauding pike badly wounded at least two more before finally taking one and settling down to enjoy its tea.

Giving the pike two days to digest his one-pound meal I returned to try again. Choosing a deep natural pool just above the spot where we had tried in vain to catch him, I threaded a dead mackerel onto two treble hooks, cast it into the pool, sat back and lit my pipe. After about ten minutes there was a twitch on my line, then nothing. After waiting a while, I gave a tug, and "wow" the pike was on. Away out of my pool, it went and down the brook with immense power. As it thrashed about in the water I saw two or three fish pushing into the weeds growing in the shallows along the banks. When the pike tired I brought it back up into my pool where it again fought with renewed strength. As it fought I could see the movement of another fish pushing into the weeds directly opposite me. I suppose it was hiding in fear from the dreaded enemy. Finally, a three pound eight ounce, female pike came onto the bank. She was in splendid condition. Although not a large fish, in this small brook and perhaps coupled with my determination to land her, that pike gave me the most exciting fifteen minutes I could wish for. Afterwards I sat quiet and watched the brook. It was about five

minutes before the fish, hiding in the weeds opposite to me, decided the danger had gone. I saw it wriggle back out to return to 'life in the mainstream'.

Towards the end of April wild primroses flower in small clumps along the valley, and in one small area on the steep bank they cascaded down to the water's edge like a drape of cream net curtains. On a pleasant sunny morning I found a comfortable seat on the opposite bank to them. With my labrador, Melle, 'we' enjoyed my lunch - well, how can you refuse the pleading look of a black labrador. Melle was watching something behind me. When I turned there was a hare on the meadow, quite close to us. From its actions, it was obviously a buck engrossed in following the scent of an in-season female. She must have had an interesting night because, nose to the ground; he meandered across the field twice, before circling round the meadow to cross the brook over the cattle bridge. Weaving his way up the bank opposite, the buck finally went over the top and out of sight.

Mad 'March' hares are usually males competing for a female, though often it is the female that boxes with a male. The spring mating ritual can take place any time from mid February through March and into April. Perhaps the female that this hare was searching for had failed to breed from her first spring activities, or maybe she had just lost her first litter. Although hares do breed again later in the year, I have seldom seen them boxing or fighting then. When the scent trail finally took this amorous buck to his chosen lady, no doubt there would be four or five others there before him. The scent of an in-season female must be very strong to entice every buck hare within a mile or more, as it does. I have seen as many as twelve together, but more often five or six will compete for the favours of one female. Unfortunately, this time their boxing antics would take place over the hill out of my sight.

"IT'S THAT TIME OF YEAR AGAIN"!

There are always some mallard ducks feeding along the brook. By late April they have usually mated, nested and hatched out a clutch of ducklings. This year there was one duck which had seemingly lost her first clutch of eggs, perhaps eaten by a fox or a mink. Whatever the reason, two drakes were competing for her favour. I had watched them earlier in the day, further down the brook, waddling about in an argumentative threesome. The two drakes finally took to the air to give an aerobatics flying display, swooping, turning and jostling each other in flight, in a way that impressed even me, let alone the female, who flew sedately along to watch.

As the month draws to a close, fly life gets more varied, but if the weather stays dull and wet, the same flies I mentioned earlier, can take me through and into May. If there are no fish moving I sometimes fish blind (my word for covering the water with a wet fly in hope of tempting a resting trout). Some use a pheasant tail nymph but I fish with a black and red nymph, or a greenish wet fly, such as an Alexandria, fishing downstream, can also give some sport. There is no need to be an entomologist to enjoy fishing in a brook, particularly in April, because fish will still be feeding on a wide variety of insects.

This early in the season, the water is still so high, you don't even need to be an expert at casting for this type of wet fly fishing. Just get the line out as straight as you can and let the current straighten out the kinks. Fish usually take on the retrieve but not always, so if you are floating a nymph down behind trees or round bends, keep the line reasonably straight or you can miss gentle takes. In fact one evening I was aware of several gentle knocks when the fly was floating downstream, but nothing when I drew it towards me. So I tried again, keeping the line as straight as possible, and "bingo", I hooked and landed a ten-ounce roach. We looked at each other with more than a little surprise.

There is no magical date for a hatch of particular flies; a couple of warm days towards the end of April can completely change the scene. Sunshine, and the resulting warmer water, soon triggers a hatch of some of the upwing flies in the olive group, which in turn brings fish up to feed nearer, if not on, the surface. I have noticed that these early olives seem to hatch in quite small numbers and from very small areas of no more than a couple yards in length - another microclimate.

It is difficult to advise on which olive dry fly is best early in the season. If you really do want to try to match them, its size and colour that is important, but I will return to them in May. A few more weeks into the year there can be such a mixture of olives and mayflies that the fish can be as confused as me.

Though water plays no part in the life cycle of the hawthorn fly, they are usually found near to it and a few drop onto the surface with a splash that excites hungry Spring trout. It is sometimes called St Mark's fly because it is more numerous around St Mark's day on April 25th. In spring, a fly box without a hawthorn tying inside, is not complete.

While sitting thinking which fly to fish with, I was thrilled to hear the laughing call of the green woodpecker. A more shy bird than the greater spotted woodpecker, they seem to like this uninhabited valley. Green woodpeckers fly in a distinctive undulating manner, a few beats of the wings, then a pause. They give their delightful call in flight, on the pause part, followed by another flutter of wings, taking them up, before a bob down and a call again on the next pause. In Derbyshire the green woodpecker's call is known as a yaffle - I think it has a nice ring to it.

The pair that I was watching seemed to have made the hole for their nest, in a dead part high in a sycamore tree (the trunk probably had its bark stripped by a grey squirrel).

"JUST HOW LONG IS THIS GOING TO TAKE?"

Although I was sure the hole was there, it was so carefully placed that, whichever angle I looked from, it was blocked from view by the leaves of overhanging branches.

Not today

Did you not touch a fish today?
No, but there was some one there who did,
He dazzled in colour like a glint of gold
And sat on a bough to dive deep and bold.
Yes, he did take a fish mid day.

Could you not stalk a fish this day?
Well there was another there who could.
Wearing a coat of grey and blue
He moved with stealth and with beak he slew.
And he was fishing without my say.

Then you've not struck a fish all day?
There was one who was quick to strike.
He is the 'jaws' of pool and brook,
Attacking from ambush, and the fish he took
He just swallowed it without delay.

My love, is there nought for tea this day?
No, but I am so full of what was there,
For song thrush, owl and wren have been,
Even fox, stoat and hare I have seen.
So my dear - just open a tin today.

4
MAY

By the first week of the month, the newly stocked fish had settled, and were enjoying their freedom. By May, both the newly stocked fish and the over wintered trout are ready for a feeding frenzy.

It is a lovely month to be at the waterside, with the colour of the new leaves, with each tree species having its own distinctive shade of pastel green. Oak leaves can vary from tree to tree; some have a deep tinge of bronze whilst others are a pale delicate green. The wild flowers are also superb now, with the primroses still in full bloom. Kingcups are usually found around ponds and marsh areas, but here we have just one large clump, growing right at the water's edge. It gives a dense patch of 'buttercup' yellow on the far bank. On the near bank, along the meadowside, cuckoo flowers (mayflower) dance in the breeze on their tall fragile stems. They look like pale lilac moths fluttering around a light, always there but never still.

With the birds in full song and full of spring activity, I find immense peace just pottering by the brook. There is a fascination in just watching the brook's many inhabitants engaged in their annual urge to re-create. It is far more than just sex; for most birds the sexual activity last but a few days Mind you it is a busy few days, but then the energy sapping task of feeding and protecting their young will last for many weeks.

Many birds will pay the price with their lives, as predators also have young to feed. A pair of greater-spotted woodpeckers, who regularly visited my garden at home, vanished this year whilst feeding their young. I know that one definitely, and the other probably, fell victim to a sparrowhawk, who himself would have had young to feed.

The grey wagtails have left the dams on the brook to move up to the farmyard. There they nest in a hole high in the old shippen wall, from where they can view the activity of the farm with interest and safety. Mr Wagtail is very protective of his territory and will not tolerate any intrusion by others of his species. This year he has a problem, his challengers come by motor car, particularly in the wing mirrors - in one day of intense activity he beat up three wing mirrors on different cars. I wonder what boastful story he told his mate that night? How at great risk and danger he defended her honour and his territory? Whatever the story, there is no doubt that he would have a sore head to back it up.

Some time later we visited another farm, and we noticed that in the farmyard was a car, which looked a bit unusual. When my wife went to investigate, she discovered that a pair of oven gloves had been cut into two and each one slipped over a wing mirror. Grey wagtails are becoming dangerous, we thought.

The early part of May can also be very frustrating for the brook fisherman, so much promise, yet cold winds, or high water, can prevent good fishing. On stocked ponds and lakes, where the water stays clean, heavy rain and cold winds just make you fish deeper. On a small brook like this, those same conditions make fly-fishing difficult if not impossible.

A phone call from Gerald, on a mild day early

in the month, drew an enthusiastic response from me, and off we went to try our luck. When we got to the water we were disappointed to find that it was very high and chocolate coloured, we had not realised how much rain there had been further across the catchment area. Undaunted we tackled up but didn't even discuss what fly may take fish, before going off to fish on different lengths. Nymphs take a lot of May trout so I tried one or two but there was no response - and I was soon bored of casting into 'liquid chocolate'.

During the time I had been at the brook I had been aware of the activities of a pair of mistle thrushes, obviously collecting grubs and worms to feed their young. They moved back and too across the meadow. So I put my rod down and wandered over to try to find the nest. Their activity was centred round a clump of half-grown oak trees (perhaps a hundred years old), which were growing near the bottom of the steep bank. I looked from the east side because mistle thrushes usually build next to the trunk and it is on the east they find their best shelter from the early summer, wet westerly winds. I did not need to walk about because I could clearly see the trunks of the five or six oaks from one place, but even after about ten minutes, there just didn't seem to be a nest in view. I was well aware though of a hen chaffinch swearing at me from the safety of the oak branches above my head, and looking into a small straggly thorn bush, right next to me, there was her nest of moss and fine fibre. The chaffinch was right to be worried because the nest was not well hidden; when the chicks hatched they would be vulnerable to a sharp eyed magpie or a grey-squirrel.

The older country folk called the noisy mistle thrush a stormcock, perhaps because they tend to sing more when rain is imminent. Now with me close to their nest, they moved away and did nothing to give the game away. In the end I wandered away but after a few minutes I returned back to the same spot and there was the nest. I had been looking right at it all the time; it was about fifteen feet above ground, on the side of a burr oak just in front of me. A stem of grass trailed out from the small wispy branches growing from one of the many burrs. I wonder if they knew the quality of their nesting site because those tiny wispy branches, growing out from burrs all the way up the trunk, will some day produce the rare burr wood highly valued in furniture making. When that tree is mature in another sixty or seventy years, I wondered, what it will be worth? - and how many birds will have by then built nests in its camouflaged shelter?

Gerald came across too see what I was up to, and to tell me about his fishing. He had caught three nice trout on a dry coachman. You may wonder as I did, why, with fast flowing coloured water, and not a trout rising, he chose that fly? His reasons were these: The coachman, always a good stand-by on this brook later in the summer, would show up well in the murky water. Not that a dry fly would float for long in such current but it would stay high in the water when retrieved against the fast flow. In fact he caught all three on the retrieve with the fly about three inches under the surface. On a small brook, which can rise and fall through the season, or even in a few hours, you have to be inventive and experiment more than you would need to on a lake.

Of course the spring water level soon falls, and by the middle of the month, more fish could be seen feeding. Although there are many different flies about the brook by now, none are in great numbers, so the choice is not easy. Some fishermen along this brook stick to nymphs or wet fly through most of May.

Mid-May can see a big hatch of alder fly, but I have had no real success fishing a dry alder. In a previous year, when there had been a good hatch of alder fly, I saw so many of the dark mottled-brown flies resting on both the trunks of the alder trees and the stems of tall water plants, I decided to just sit and watch them. They live for two years in the water before the larva crawl out to turn into pupae in the mud by the waterside. Although there are artificial patterns to imitate the larva I have yet to have success with them. During the time it took for Melle and me to empty my sandwich box, not one alder fly took to the wing over land or water, nor for that matter did one fish move. In fact the only action was from the dog - she ate too large a share of my tea. The only time in May that I have thought that alders could come into my dry fly fishing, has been at late dusk, when I have seen large fish taking insects from in the edge of the grass along the banks. I presumed they were taking the alder flies as they laid their eggs on the leaves of water grass lying on the surface.

The caddis flies are not really active until a bit later in the summer and mostly at night. However their larvae are in the water, so when all else fails, I try to match these. But the larvae have to pupate (see June) and it is at this stage, which lasts a couple of weeks, that the caddis becomes more interesting to the fisherman. Although we all fish with just one fly and no droppers, on a small river such as this, with so many snags, it is easy enough to loose even a single fly, but one is enough. Which fly you use is not as important as how you use it. With trees and bends there is not the space to fish with a long rod; seven to eight feet seems to be the best length here, and as the cast has to be proportionate to rod length then there certainly is not room for two droppers. There is no need for either a sinking line or a heavy line to cast long distances, in fact I only use a floating line with just one fly. Whatever line you use, it must land gently.

Although there are more olives hatching in

the second half of the month, before I tell you about them, I feel I must sidetrack and tell you about my cat. It is white and like most white cats with blue eyes, it is completely deaf. A cat with both a pink eye and a blue one will hear on the pink side and be deaf on the blue. My deaf cat's sensitivity through its feet is quite remarkable.

I often take a walk in the wood behind my home with both Melle and the cat. If the cat gets left behind I signal to it by giving three bumps on the ground with my walking stick. On a bare path the cat can feel that signal at forty paces. I have even tried hiding among the bushes but this deaf cat turns towards my signal without hesitation - which seems to prove that the cat not only feels the signal through her paws, but also

senses the direction with complete accuracy. So I ask you, how much more can a trout feel, with its acute senses, and in water which carries every vibration?

If you need an example of how to move, around water, just sit and watch a heron, a master fisherman, who lives or dies by his fishing skills. Just remember that he has been perfecting his technique through the odd million years. The heron stands still for long periods; if he moves at all, it is with a gentle slowness. His camouflage is blue/grey against the colour of sky, his body is his rod, his neck is his line and his beak his hook - in all only a couple of feet in length - yet he can spear some of the largest trout in the brook - the rogue!

I have watched men, wearing a white shirt, approach a stocked pond with a thumping walk, and immediately wade in to cast a great length of line towards some distant fish. That happened once when I had my nine-year-old daughter with me, and she asked, *"Dad does that make sense?"* On a small brook you need to get in close to the fish, so before casting a line, stand back from the water and watch - then watch a little longer. When you decide where a fish might be, plan your approach to stay off the skyline. Move slowly and, if the sun is out, be careful to keep your shadow off the water.

If you were to use the same method on still water you could take trout right by the bank. In fact when I watched one of my fishing companions, Richard Smith, fish a small lake, his approach was with that same caution. Staying well back from the waterside, he covered the shallows just in from the grassy bank, before walking quietly to the water's edge. Even then he cast only a 'shortish' line just in from, and parallel to, the bank side, before covering the open water. The reason fish seem to feed along way away, is usually because your activity has sent them there, or at least sent those close to you into hiding.

Sunshine in late May brings out the first hatch of small tortoiseshell butterflies. Small tortoiseshell love wild flowers and flit from one to another. One day when I was taking a rest to watch them, I was sitting low among the rushes and a kingfisher came to perch on a twig on the opposite bank to me. When it dived in I could not see what it caught, I presumed

Small Tortoiseshell

that whatever it was it was so small that it did not protrude out of the birds beak. Certainly there was no head banging on the branch sequel; it just landed back on the perch, gave a quick flick of its feathers and flew away to return again within minutes. I am not sure that I can tell male from female, but one or the other came every few minutes to the same perch, sat for a few seconds, then took a deep dive to catch whatever again? I could only presume it was either very small fry or some kind of insect suitably sized for their very young chicks. Two days later I returned with my field glasses determined to see what they were taking. I sat hidden in the same spot for more than an hour and never even saw a kingfisher. Such is nature.

The sunshine also gets the dairy farmers excited. Silage is made from much younger grass than hay. Rain, causing a few days delay in cutting spring grass, can dramatically increase its fibre content and reduce its feed value. Although farmers do not require the days of sunshine that was needed for hay making, silage is much better if the weather is dry. Sunshine brings sugar up into the grass leaf, which in turn produces the right fermentation in the final product. Making silage in wet weather increases the dangerous effluent, which has to be disposed of, and encourages the wrong type of acids in the cows' diet. The difference between good and poor silage can be many thousands, if not teens of thousands of pounds, to a dairy farmer. It is no wonder they get a bit excited around the 20th May. Travelling past several dairy farms, on my journey to the brook, was an interesting, if not dangerous, journey. The urge to cart the silage in before nightfall seemed to be quite equal to that of any wild bird's urge to recreate and feed their young.

In places along the meadow side of the brook, pignuts (umbellifera family) grow; as children we used to dig them up to eat them. The small head of white flowers on a short twelve-inch stem is quite insignificant to look at, but at the bottom of each flower stem is a bulb, or nut to country children, that is pleasant to eat. Here the badgers have learned how to dig them up in one sandy spot along the bank, rooting up small patches of grassland to get at the delicacy. I could not resist trying to recapture my childhood, so I dug a few for myself, but 'they didn't taste like they used to', so I left the rest for the badgers.

Upwing flies come in various sizes, but in only one basic shape - which is a upward curving body, upright wings and two or three (according to species) long tails. Fishing books go into minute detail as to the identification of each fly, but this is not that sort of book. Although both olives and mayflies are slowly returning to the brook, they still do not hatch in the large numbers of yester years, but there are still a few different species present.

When choosing a matching artificial, size matters more than individual identification, as to which olives or mayfly are hatching at any one time. If you really want to identify each fly then there are many books to choose from, I use *John Goddard's Waterside Guide*, but I don't believe it is necessary. Just fish a hackled grey/green dry fly such as a grey duster or a grey wolf. With so many other olive and dun imitations available, advice on selection can be confusing; mine is always to choose from a hackled tying rather than a winged one. Presentation and field craft are much more important on a small river or brook than choice of fly.

One evening I was invited to fish a different length of this brook. Another guest there was fishing a Wickam's Fancy, and when I asked him why? His reply was, *"I always fish this one fly right through the season, it rides high in the water and will take both rising trout and tempt those feeding lower down".* I am not suggesting myself quite that you only need to fish just one fly, but I know good brook fly fishermen who use no more than four or five flies throughout the season. There is a lot of nonsense talked by people whose real aim is to sell another fishing book or to tempt you to buy a new 'marvellous' fly.

Mayfly have returned to our length of brook after many years through which I hardly knew what a mayfly was. I can only presume the water is cleaner and insects that have been affected by pollution and the soft sand, are now themselves breeding again. June is really the month of the mayfly - it is because in the old British calendar, when the fly was given its name - May came about ten days later than now. Even so it is well worth trying a mayfly nymph near the end of the month and even into early June. Until the hatch is really on, fish seem cautious of taking a large dry mayfly but they will often take a nymph fished high in the water.

You must be wondering what has happened to Bill this month, perhaps I should explain. This book is mainly about our fishing in one year, although some of the wildlife stories are borrowed from previous years. In May of that year Bill and I only fished together once, and then he was late:

"Guilty of arriving late to fish!"

"What have you got to say in your defence before I pass sentence"?

"Well, it was like this my Lord, I was held up by some geese".

Bill's journey takes him along some narrow country lanes. When he was travelling along one of these, a family of wild Canada geese came onto the road just in front of him. Mum, Dad and their young family then proceeded down the lane at a leisurely pace, and would not be diverted. Bill jumped out of the car and tried hard to turn them into different fields, but to no avail. In the end, he just relaxed and enjoyed the experience. The geese finally came to their chosen gateway, a pasture field with a large pond in the centre, and off they went.

5
JUNE

On the first day of June I had invited my brother Arthur to fish with me. Arriving a little early on a beautiful sunny morning and, not being in a hurry to fish, I just sat amongst the flowers on the meadow bank enjoying the sunshine. Surprisingly there was no fish moving but the flowers were superb. Although the primroses had faded away on the steep bank opposite me, now part of it was bathed in the less dense clothing of white flowers of the greater stitchwort. Around me buttercups had joined the white pignuts and the last of the cuckoo flowers.

Several small white butterflies were about, and also one that I believe might be a large skipper. It was not hard though to identify the male orange tip butterflies when they came dancing along the brook sides. Cuckoo flowers are the favourite plant for the

orange tip to lay their eggs. It is cause for concern that there are but just a few growing along this brookside, and almost none elsewhere on the farm.

When Arthur came along the brook bank towards me, his first comments were not about fishing but about a bird singing among the thorn bushes close by. My guess had been that it was a blackcap but Arthur, explaining the subtle difference in the song of each bird, said it was a garden warbler. Well even then I wasn't sure. Maybe I have to accept that my ear is just not good enough to detect the difference - but I do know that little bird could certainly make music.

There are some 190 species of caddisfly, and they have a variety of ways to camouflage or hide their larvae, particularly when they reach pupation. When that time comes they seal the larval case with a variety of substances from moss to gravel. I studied the colour of our grit covered caddis larvae; they look a bit like a rubbish tip in the corner of a builders yard.

It is at the pupae stage, when the different species are on the move, that the fisherman should take an interest. Some species travel towards the shore to find a way of climbing to the surface while others hatch out at the surface in open water. On this brook, I have found that fishing in mid water with a pupae look-alike, seems to work. The disabilities in my fingers make fly tying too difficult, so I asked a friend, who enjoys a challenge, to create a wet fly to match

our caddis larvae. Jim Wilson, from Hertford, came up with several variations and surprisingly they all took fish. We finally fixed on one that is on the lines of, but quite distinct, from a bibio, which he named the Peover Aye Aye. It has black and red seal fur dubbing with silver rib, a ginger game hackle and a short red tail. But my description doesn't do it credit. If you wish to try to tie one use a pale red, the colour of Cheshire brick will do, then tie two bands of Cheshire brick red to break up the black of the body.

With no fish moving on the surface Arthur chose this fly and within minutes netted a nice trout. Finally a fish did move some forty yards upstream, and Arthur quietly moved towards it. Casting up stream he took the fish on the first cast.

Anglers know the adult caddisfly as sedge. The fact that they fly mostly in the late evening or at night means that seldom is there a sufficient number over the water to get either the trout or the fisherman excited. On a lake the hatch may be different than here, perhaps there the wind may blow larger numbers over the water. On a narrow brook, a fly is often just blown from one bank to the other. Even so, in the late evening, sedge imitation is worth a try from June through to late August. Although I will say more about them in July - this early in the season I find that a size 12 pale ginger or light brown fly seem to take, but don't hold your breath!

We call the larger, up-wing flies, mayflies, but some like to differentiate between the green drake, which is the true mayfly and some of the larger species of olives. If you want to be technical - the larger olives have only two tails as against the three of the mayfly and of course they are slightly smaller. But I think, what does it matter, let's get to the brook-side and fish.

By the tenth of June this year the mayfly hatch was in full swing. I had bought two rough olive mayflies and fished them through the month and well into July. In fact I lent one of them to two different friends who were with me; both flies took a good number of trout and are still in my fly box at the end of the season. I get better results from a hackled dry fly (those fancy winged tyings are to catch fishermen) - hackled flies float better and take more fish. In fact they may take several fish without needing to be changed.

The year before, on one evening, I hooked nine fish. Although I only succeeded in landing five of them, they were all on the same hackled dry fly that had still floated in the surface film to take the last of those nine trout. The fact that it all happened in an hour and five minutes made it a night to remember. (Here I must confess that I tend to forget the times I have lost two or three flies without even one fish on the bank). I have not told you which fly it was and I can't, simple because I don't know. Taking it off after that ninth trout, I hooked it in the lamb's wool patch on my fishing waistcoat -and lost it! I didn't have another like it! I have looked for a similar one in tackle shops without success. There seems to be a fashion to tie hackled mayfly and olives with divided hackles to give an impression of wings - leave them alone - go for a bristly mop head tying.

Whichever dry fly I decide to use, I try to cast upstream to the rising fish, simply because it is the best and most enjoyable way to take trout. The three main reasons in favour of up stream casting are: Firstly trout lie mainly facing upstream, so it makes sense to creep up behind them. Secondly if there is no take, the fly floats gently back down below the fish lie, where you can then lift it without disturbing the feeding trout. Thirdly it is harder to present a dry fly either down stream or across the flow, because, unless the fish takes the fly on the drop, the current will sweep the leader sideways, which drags the fly in an unnatural manner. Anything looking slightly unnatural alerts most wary fish.

When casting upstream I try to drop the fly just short of the fish, making him turn to take it and if he does not, I just extend the line another foot and try again. Even though a dry fly needs to land with the least disturbance possible, just as a real fly would - trout can easily feel it touch down behind them. Over-casting can show what the fly is attached to, which is a turn off for most fish. In fact if I have to cast a dry fly down stream for whatever reason, I still drop it short of the fish. But casting across the flow I try to put the fly nearer to the fish in the hope that it will take on the drop before the current creates a drag. In a small brook fish usually feed in water that is only about a foot deep, so the movement of a line dragging on the surface, whatever its colour, is a certain put down.

Chatting to the farmer, one day in mid June, he told me an amusing story that had happened only that morning, when he was looking around his sheep. Like most modern farmers he now dashes round his fields on a quad bike, and there is a seat on the back for the faithful collie. Modern sheep dogs, it seems, no longer run, but spend most of their life sitting on

G.AshleyHunter

Wickham's Fancy
Grey Duster
Hawthorn
Coachman
Alexandra

the back of a quad bike. That morning they had startled a heron from where it had been quietly fishing in the brook. In its rush to get away the heron flew close to the nesting carrion crows, and they immediately attacked. Although they were only making mock attacks, they were real enough to cause the heron to panic. Ducking and weaving in fear, the heron dropped a fish in his bid to escape. When the farmer drove across there he found a trout of about a pound in weight. It is probable that the heron had not completely swallowed the fish when it was frightened up from the water - I suppose that it takes

"LIFE WILL NEVER BE THE SAME NOW SHEP HAS GONE MECHANIZED"

some time to swallow a fish of that size down the length of a heron's neck.

Although there is only one clump of wild iris along our length of brook, it is a large one. It is in fact slowly slipping into the water and causing a narrow channel, which in turn creates a whirlpool of some depth. The effect of the swirl of water has collapsed the bank on the meadow side, leaving a vertical ten foot face of sand making it difficult for me to get below to cast up into the pool, so I usually stand by the iris clump and cast down stream. One day, with two trout feeding in the pool, with one clumsy cast I managed to frighten both. When I have put a fish down like that, I often stop casting, sit down quietly and wait. Within ten to twenty minutes most fish will begin to feed again and if they do, I am ready in position to cast to them without moving. Why walk away when you know that there is a hungry fish right in front of you?

I sat with Melle, by the water, with a high grass high bank behind and the ten-foot high sand face to my right. Although I thought of changing flies, instead I became fascinated by the activities of a pair of wrens. They were obviously feeding young; even watching them from so close it took a while to work out where their nest was. It was in a small fold of turf at the very top of the steep sand face where the soil had fallen and exposed the roots of the pasture grass, which had then curled down. In fact, as I watched, a cow grazed grass from the very roof of the tiny nest. The wrens themselves were back and too with a selection of insects, mostly caught out of a bog of nettles just across the brook. On alternate journeys, one wren (the cock I presume), let on a post on the far bank to give a little burst of song. On one return trip he had a daddy-long-legs head first in his beak, and on each side of his face the daddy's wings stuck up and out, giving the effect of a pair of sun glasses, its legs trailing below, each side of the beak. It was hard to tell who should have caught whom but that cheeky little bird, with what to him was a massive insect in his beak, still let on the post and gave his burst of song.

SOMETHING TO SING ABOUT

Eventually a trout did start to feed again. I cast from where I sat, but I 'over' cast and put it straight off again. So waiting does not always work, although if I had not sat still I would not have seen the wren. Much of the material for this book has come from observations when doing just that.

As it was a pleasant afternoon, Melle and I wandered back up the brook, to look for more action. I saw another fish feeding and, after a careful approach, 'over' cast again. These fish, after a week or two in the brook, become as wild as their ancestors ever were, so now after two months -or two years in the case of the larger fish - they are very wary; the sight of a leader or line landing - however lightly - over their nose, will send them into hiding as quick as anything. I told myself to write a hundred lines. "I must not over cast. I must not over cast. - I must not...." I went home with out a fish, perhaps that's punishment enough.

Most fishing books I read are full of scientific facts and diagrams. I am trying hard to avoid both but a little knowledge helps some times. Some years ago, when fishing a small private lake, there was no trout rising other than in one small area by the bank. I slid down the steep bank, within a short casting distance from the two or three feeding trout, but I still couldn't make out what they were feeding on. It was some ten minutes before I did and it was so simple. There were numerous small half inch green caterpillars, suspended from the over-hanging oak boughs, on very fine silk threads.

The green oak tortrix moths lay their eggs on the twigs of oak trees, timed to hatch out in spring to eat inside the new buds. As the caterpillars grow they not only feed on the young oak leaves but curl the leaves up into a small tube shaped den, which is neatly tied with the caterpillars silk, and the caterpillars hide and pupate within that leaf ball. I used to think the dangling caterpillars were coming down to ground to pupate, but not so. It is only when they are disturbed by predators, i.e. by small birds or hunting ants, that they do a quick bungee jump, to hang suspended until all is clear. If you put your self in their place, it may not be easy to get the calculations just right with an ant nibbling at your tummy button and twenty of his mates closing in from all sides. You might just forget that you have doubled your body weight since the last jump. Whatever the reason, enough were getting it wrong over the water to get those trout moving. I quickly rooted through my fly box for something green that looked like a caterpillar; with three casts I caught two brownies, each at one and half pounds, and as like as peas in a pod.

We noted earlier that there is about a thousand insect species on an oak tree; of those there is about a hundred different species of butterflies and moths dependant on the oak at some time in their life cycle. If you think about that then you realise that almost any thing can drop out throughout the season. Our oaks are mostly separated from the water by the alder and hawthorn but there is one oak in particular that hangs clear of obstruction over the brook. In late June enough caterpillars were miscalculating their bungee jumps to give me an hour of good sport under it with a green caterpillar/nymph.

6
JULY

By July the days can be very hot, which in turn warms the water up. Then trout become less active, particularly through the heat of the afternoon. Evenings are now the most promising time to fish. I usually try to arrive at the brook by about 5.00pm. When there is a guest with me and if (as is usual) the fish are not moving, we just sit and chat over a relaxed tea until the fish also start to feed.

If there is just Melle and myself, we sit and munch the food, watching the life of the little valley going on around us. As Melle always sits fairly close to me, even when there is no food, I am often surprised how much wildlife she is aware off before I am. We have spent many hours together waiting for ducks or pigeons, so she is always watching the sky, but it is more than that. Dogs have much more acute senses than we have, both their hearing and sense of smell are far beyond our own.

An alert and experienced shooting dog, sitting quietly with you, can considerable increase what you see. Whatever I am doing, whether it's fishing, shooting or just pottering about in the countryside, I try to keep my dog's face in the corner of my eye. When she fixes her gaze I follow it. She has a bad habit of wagging her tail when duck are overhead but other than that she is steady. Melle will sit quietly watching rabbits playing nearby; even a badger has come within twenty metres of us. At the sight of a fox though, all self-control breaks down, and - unless I can put my hand on her - the fox has to leg it quick.

On those warm days, throughout July and August, there is usually a special evening rise at dusk time, and at that time there can be a good movement of fish. Some times it only lasts ten minutes, at others an exciting hour. I usually fish through the early evening. At about eight I have a break, get out the tea flask and look over my tackle in preparation for this magical evening rise.

Because the bigger fish often move in this short period of excitement, I want the right fly on and dressed ready to cast. I then actually sit by the water and wait. But this year it never happened. Each evening I was at the brook, just when the adrenaline was beginning to flow with expectation, a cold breeze came down the valley and the brook went dead. There must have been other nights when the weather combination was right, bringing the fish onto feed at dusk, but if there were, I missed them.

Sitting by the brook, rod in hand, waiting for something that just did not happen, gave me time for reflection. I noticed there were a good number of rabbits along the meadow, so I enjoyed watching them, frolicking and skipping, as they ventured further across the meadow in the fading light. Even though the rabbits were with us all summer I never saw a stoat, and with that number of rabbits, it was surprising. On reflection I realised that the number of stoats seen in the fields along this watercourse has fallen dramatically in the last few years, in fact, not just here, but also around my own farm. This is nothing to do with the dreaded disease in rabbits; myxomatosis has been around for over forty years but the drop in the stoat population seems to have taken place from around 1990.

It is during the years since then that the mink

population has exploded in our countryside. When a completely new predator moves in, and in such large numbers, the existing wildlife have no time to adapt. Normally evolution would allow a species to adapt to the gradual migration of a new carnivore, but for that they need the odd thousand if not millions of years. Already mink have wiped out all the lovely furry water voles along this brook. I mourn the passing of these innocent little animals and blame those stupid activists who are guilty of releasing such indiscriminate killers in our countryside. It's not just animals that have been affected. Mink have dramatically reduced both the waterhen and nesting ducks along this and other water courses. Not many

people - even country people - realise the numbers of mink or the damage done by them.

I visited one house along the brook where they keep some rare water birds. To help protect those ducks from marauding mink the owners have to keep a cage set near to the pens. In eight years they have caught 108 mink. Think of the wild life devastation that extra number would have caused along this little river valley had they lived. We often see mink hunting well away from any main watercourse, which leads me to believe that they are responsible for the fall in the numbers of our native stoats. There is no doubt that with their extra strength and speed a mink could kill a stoat.

Gerald was fishing the lower length when he met a family of mink cutting across the meadow from one brook bend to the next. The larger male faced up to him for the few seconds that it took for mum and the young to dash back to the water. When I repeated that story to country friends they cast doubt, not on the fact that a mink would face up to a man, but that a male would be hunting alongside a female with young. Most country people like to see for themselves! Each time I have told of seeing a pair of stoats, not just hunting together, but also actually hunting to a plan, that story has also met with a doubting silence.

It happened when fishing the same small lake

where I first noticed the dangling caterpillars. Standing quietly under an oak tree watching the water, I became aware of a mallard duck with a brood of young suddenly becoming agitated. The ducks, swimming in a narrow stretch of water, were panicking away from the far bank. I looked up and there in an open spot on the bank, some three feet above the water, was a large male stoat. With head back he was literally flashing the white on his breast. Because of the narrowness of the water there the ducks were being driven by fear towards my bank. When I looked there, in among the rushes, a smaller female stoat was scuttling into ambush position. Unfortunately a small bush blocked my view of the spot where she would meet the ducks. I moved to see the outcome but alas one or other stoat detected me and both of them vanished into the vegetation. I stopped recounting that incident when I met with scepticism. Since then apparently something similarly has been shown on TV - so now it is alright to believe it!

While working on this book I heard rumours of an otter. Dismissing them as imaginative mink sightings, they were put out of my mind. Later though I questioned a local countryman who declared that he had in fact seen an otter crossing the road on a bridge over the Peover Eye. As he had seen otters in the wild when fishing both on the Eden in Cumbria, and in Scotland, I have no reason to

doubt him. Otters need to wander the banks of each river from coast to source. If they are to return to the Peover Eye they will need to learn how to negotiate their way round Winnington Chemical works before facing the polluted Mersey Estuary. Where this otter came from or where it went to will remain a mystery. I wonder - will I live to see that beautiful creature swimming under my rod?

The aerobatic flying display given by the two mallard drakes in April must have been successful-for one of them at least, because there was a late hatch of ducklings on the brook. I enjoyed watching them bobbing down the small dams. On the way up mum climbed out onto the bank to lead them round the fast water but going down they seemed to enjoy the thrill of shooting the rapids. The current swept them down, at times sideways, sometimes even backwards; through it they sat as lightly on the water as blobs of thistle down. At the bottom the happy little group all chased after another insect in a flurry of competition and fun.

In this particular year I have seldom fished without a sight of a kingfisher, mostly just a flash of turquoise blue as it flew past just above the water. Other than the one episode earlier in the year, none of us had had a chance to watch them for any length of time. A few years ago, Gerald was casting across the stream to a rising trout; at the moment when his fly covered the fish - as he held his breath with rod horizontal anticipating the strike of the trout - a kingfisher let on his rod. Both he and the bird looked at each other in a moment of amazement, and then the little bird flew on its way.

My own similar experience was on the small lake mentioned before. Sitting down to rest from fishing I put my rod down on a clump of rushes, leaving it leaning out over the water. The dog was sitting tight by my side when a kingfisher landed about half way along the rod. I stayed absolutely still whilst that lovely bird looked, first down into the water, then back at me. This seemed to go on for ages, but in reality only for a brief minute, before the dog snapped at an annoying fly and the spell was broken. But I am still waiting for the same thing to happen to me on this brook.

The fishing can be poor in late July. Usually fish are feeding but it needs plenty of hard work to take them, although in a year like this one with a good hatch of mayfly it is relatively simple. I just fished the same hackled mayfly from June through to about the tenth of the month and then I dropped down a size to a smaller olive. Although there are times when I have had to search for a rising fish, or perhaps even wait for one to get hungry. As I have said, I am convinced that the variance here in upwing fly numbers is caused by silica sand smothering the eggs

and nymphs; but perhaps this is not the right place to whinge about it.

At other times there is still the sedge or caddis to tempt a fish to rise. As I have already mentioned, most of the larvae in this group of species (trichoptera), spend their life crawling around on or close to the river bed. Some species swim up to hatch on the surface whilst others swim to the sides to then climb and cling to vegetation while they emerge from the pupae case. From mid-June, and through July, fish seem to take some of those pupae from the lip of the dams. Perhaps as they are heading towards the bank the drag of water draws them up before it flows over the top. In past years I have taken a few fish by casting down stream to drop a nymph on the very lip of a dam.

When that method fails there is still the

chance of an evening hatch but as most species of sedge crawl up the stalk of a brookside plant to hatch, there is not much to see. I had fished a coachman here for a few years before realising that may be I was matching the sedge. In the evening I often saw what I thought were small pale, almost whitish winged, moths flitting along the meadow by the brook.

The experts say that there is not a white-winged sedge but there are quite pale ones. The same experts say that if you need to identify which is which, the wings of a moth are covered with tiny scales where as those of a sedge-fly are covered with tiny hairs - but first you have to catch the things. As they move quicker than me, why bother? Just presume that any small light coloured moth-like insect along the brookside in the evening is a sedge, and fish accordingly. There is never any number, so you could use the earlier season sedge, but once I see one of those near white wings flitting along, I dig out my Coachman wet fly. Although I have taken fish on both a dry coachman and a dry royal coachman I still get the best response from a wet fly. Casting up stream to a rising fish, just as with a dry fly, the wet coachman will usually be taken as the fly hits the water. It seems that a sedge fly can live for several weeks, which makes it worth trying a sedge into late August.

The most beautiful resident insect on this brook is a large damselfly. I have to confess that, as it was not in my insect book, the first year fishing this length I did not know what it was. In fact because of its vivid colour and its habit of resting with wings held vertical like those of a butterfly, I was not even sure it was a damselfly. A fishing friend, David Mullins, who is blessed with a more extensive reference book, finally identified these splendid insects for me. The banded demoiselle damselfly is one of the two largest of the species, with a wingspan of up to 60mm. The male has a large blue patch on each of its four wings and a polished looking blue-green body, whilst the female's wings are a metallic green, without a blue patch. Although I believe they are not uncommon, I have yet to see another colony in this area of Cheshire, but I am sure there must be more.

These beautiful insects, only found along the one short stretch of open brook, do not seem to wander like other damselflies. On a sunny afternoon in July there can sometimes be up to a hundred active at any one time.

Along the length that they occupy, a type of water grass grows out from the water's edge, lying horizontally across the surface. Although this grass dies off in winter, by August it can be up to a metre in length and of course reaching in from both banks, it severely restricts our fishing. For two years we dragged a lot of this grass out onto the bank. Then on the third year we realised that our lovely damselflies were dramatically reduced in numbers. For my part I felt like a vandal, I was appalled at the damage I had so carelessly caused. Now we only remove the grass from very short lengths of brook to allow us to fish in favoured spots, whilst leaving plenty of grass for the insects to complete their matrimonial duties.

I have not identified the type of grass, but it is obvious that the life cycle of this particular damselfly is dependant on it here. The female lays her eggs within the stem of the plant, after first making a slit with her saw-like ovipositor (I looked that up in a book). After the eggs hatch they drop into the water to spend two years as a nymph before climbing up the same water plant to shed their nymphal case. It is now obvious that by dragging out the grass in late summer we were also removing the eggs from over the water. We will happily have our fishing restricted for the pleasure of the company of this most colourful of all damselflies. The good news is that their numbers have increased again but they are also vulnerable to the drifting sand.

Some fish nose into the floating grass to take the adult damselfly when they are laying their eggs. It seems to be usually at late dusk when it is hard to see for sure just what is happening. It is worth trying an artificial damsel but I find that you need to be able to cast within inches of the edge of the floating grass. Alas I seem to drop the fly a bit too far out, which catches nothing or a bit too far in, which just hooks the grass. Either way doesn't take fish!

I seem to be giving the impression that fly-fishing on this brook in July is a doddle; well it isn't. In fact some years from mid-July through to mid August both trout and the usual flies seem to take a long summer holiday. Anyway, that is how it seems when you search along the banks without seeing a trace of a fish.

A couple of years ago when the brook life seemed to stop I was also struggling with a trapped nerve. There was no way that I could walk and cast away from one end of our stretch to the other - so I did just what our rules allow - I enjoyed myself, by just staggering over to a favoured spot and sitting down rod in hand! When nothing responded to my choice of fly - a couple of maggots were added. As you fly-fishermen would expect, there was a national outcry, questions were asked in parliament and my two fishing partners gave me a right ribbing. Bill, having christened them 'my flying maggots' reminded me of my sins, months later, with a suitable Christmas card.

What I did learn though was that our trout were still there. On one completely dead afternoon, after trying an assortment of what I thought were suitable flies, I hooked on two maggots and took three trout from the very same spot without getting off my lazy bum.

"WHAT! NO FLYING MAGGOT
TODAY THEN?"

The bird life along the brook changes by late July. By now most have reared young and, according to the species, the young are at various stages of independence. The grey wagtails had moved back to the brook; having nested successfully in the farmyard they were now strutting about on the dams, young and old catching insects with their usual flurry of wings. By this time there is a need to build up body reserves.

On one visit in mid July the young carrion crows, having flown the nest, were flying about somewhat clumsily. The old country men used to call them 'flappers'. This describes perfectly how the young crows, when on early flying ventures, crash land onto the outer leafy branches of a tree. There they flap their wings desperately whilst trying to get a grip on the branch with their feet. This takes place with a lot of noisy encouragement from mum and dad, plus a chorus of frightened calls from the three or four juniors. The racket makes a complete contrast to their secret quietness whilst the young were still in the nest.

7
AUGUST

For a few years now, my early August fishing was interrupted by Macclesfield Sheepdog Society's annual trials. Not that I was directly involved, but as a member of the Midland County Stickmakers I usually helped with the stickmaking demonstration on the Friday, and also tried my skill in the stick show on the Saturday. Putting a few sticks together for the demonstration, plus polishing a few for the show, seemed to demand all of my time. For several years, Marion Yarwood, the then show secretary, also made use of Bill's talents to enhance the societies paperwork - here are some examples.

Macclesfield
& District
SHEEP
DOG
TRIALS

Macclesfield
& District
SHEEP
DOG
TRIALS
STICK JUDGE
Ash
Ash

Trees butting into a small brook can create features that considerable improves the water for fish. We have one large oak that almost grows out of the water, causing a swirl in front of it, and then where the flow goes past fast, the water has cut a deep channel which in turn makes a nice little slack eddy behind the tree. About nine feet along the bank, behind the oak, a small alder, managing to get enough light to live, straggles upwards into the lower oak branches. Then growing high into that alder is a wild honeysuckle; it's the only one along our length, so we really care for it. When we were spring-cleaning, Bill thought the alder roots were getting too long and went in to give them a trim. It is quite deep there, which meant that he was sawing roots well under water. Gerald meanwhile was trimming an overhead branch nearby, when, suddenly, and pointing towards Bill, he called out in anguish, "The honeysuckle is trembling". We all joined in the next few minutes of banter, with remarks like "Well you'd tremble if someone was sawing through your ankle".

When it was young, the honeysuckle must have climbed up then slipped back down the trunk of the alder while still coiled around it. The result is that the lovely old plant has a long loop of trunk under water, and Bill was cutting it in mistake for a root. Fortunately he stopped just in the nick of time, and I am pleased to report that it still flowered that summer. The lower branches on the honeysuckle just skim the water right over the spot of slack water behind the large oak. We don't cut these off because often one or two trout can be feeding there when the rest of the brook seems dead.

After driving across Cheshire on business I called in at the brook on the way home. My rod was in the boot as usual but unfortunately Melle was not. Wandering along the meadow there was not a fish moving until the honeysuckle came in view. What those couple of fish there were taking, was not clear, perhaps some insect falling from the large oak overhead or even from the honeysuckle. Rising right under those low scented branches, it meant there was no way to put a fly right up to them. The fast current, which swung from the oak tree across the stream towards my bank, made it impossible to float a fly to them. The only way I could cover them with a dry fly was to cast across, bending the leader at right angles down stream. Hopefully then the current would take the fly the two or three feet needed to get it under the bush before the line was swept away. If you want a dry fly to flow to a fish, then the leader must lie along the flow of the stream if the fly is to look real to the waiting trout.

Like most fishermen, I found out by accident that when I was trying hard to cast in a straight line, a leader and fly could drop short to the left, or to the right, then it would float to where I wanted it. So long ago I decided that, either floating a dry fly on flowing water, or dropping it in a difficult corner, it was useful to make that side drop into an intentional cast. It's all in the very last hand movement in your cast; try to end it a tiny bit weak and short. Although I am telling you how, there is really no way I would try to demonstrate it - but the benefits though from trying it far out way any disadvantages. If the line goes out straight by mistake, or even to the wrong side, (in a breeze!) the leader and fly land well away from the chosen fish, you just pick up and try again. There are some who claim to bend their cast either way at will; well, if they can, well done! For me, it's still too often an untidy splash that is better done without an audience.

But to get back to those trout under Bill's honeysuckle, with so many trees and bushes around that bend in the brook, there was only one spot from which I could do my 'bent' cast. Even then to get in place without being seen I had to slide down a ten-foot steep bank and cast from a sitting position at the bottom. I was completely engrossed in my second or third try, when there was a large splash to my left and a buzzard rose, seemingly straight out of the water, no more than five paces from me. I was so startled that such a large a bird could swing under the outer branches of the oak so close, and yet so silently, that I had heard nothing. Had Melle been with me, I am sure she would not have missed its coming. What it was doing I will never know; certainly it was wet right up its thighs and its great talons were dripping water as it rose from the brook. Had it been earlier in the year I would say it was collecting water in its feathers to damp the eggs in the nest - softening the shells as the chicks came close to hatching. Never having heard of a buzzard catching trout, I am not saying this one was, but it was an interesting way to take a drink!

The beauty of fishing, mostly on my own, is that I can sit and daydream without embarrassment. This time it went along these lines: Isn't it interesting that birds of prey know just what time of year to nest to match the maximum food for the chicks; they know to turn their eggs in the nest, then to soften the shells near to hatching by wetting them. The male not only understands his duty to feed his mate throughout this time but goes on to feed and fight for his family until they can fend for themselves. None of this is learned by example, but purely from genetic instinct. Modern humans have twenty or more years to observe and learn how to rear their children. Dozens of health visitors, social workers, doctors and nurses give advice and still many parents seem to make a complete hash of what in nature seems so simple, and natural, a task.

Needless to say, with all that deep daydreaming, I did not catch the trout!

A straight, neatly cleaned brook will not hold many fish; yes I know I have already told you this but it is worth repeating. Far too many fishermen want obstacle free water, whilst the trout want somewhere to call home. A fish needs some feature that makes him feel safe and as there are almost no rocks here, it has to be a root or a dead branch in the water. Even shade from something growing just above the water, can give that extra feeling of security. But the trouble in August is that there can be too much cover for the fish, both in the water and over it. We try to leave the banks to the cows but unfortunately they don't eat everything that grows; nettles, thistle and even rosebay willow herb can make fishing very difficult. As they grow taller these weeds tend to lean out over the water and interfere with casting. Walking with a stick means I have a useful tool with which to keep the bank, we fish from, reasonably free of these taller weeds. But the far bank, particularly where it is very steep, can get a lot of cover on it.

I was down at the brook in mid August, on a dull afternoon, hoping that there would have been a few fish on the move but it was not so. It was one of the few times that summer when I was reduced to trying a wet fly, in fact I tried a few, then just before I left for home I put on a size 14 un-named nymph, a gift from a fly-tying friend, but again without success. Already late for home I was actually walking back to my car when a fish moved. It was in a narrow channel, made even narrower because, from my bank, the damsel grass (as I call it) reached out on to the water for most of a metre, whilst on the opposite steep bank, tall nettles, out of reach of my walking stick, bent low over the water.

The trout was feeding under the heads of those nettles, so using the same nymph, I just cast up stream to it. I tried a slow retrieve, a fast retrieve, both shallow and deeper, all with no success. Then I did what I should have done in the first place, and I just stood still, to watch and think. The fish moved again without breaking the surface right by a spot where three nettles heads, bound together,

just touched the water. Guessing that the trout was lying under them, it was obvious I had to do something different. My only hope was to bend the cast and drop my fly into a small gap behind him. My luck held and the fish turned on the proverbial sixpence to take the fly before it had chance to sink.

It was only a pound but it gave me so much pleasure because that one fish illustrated two of the points I had learnt over the years and have tried to make through this book; the need for cover to hold fish, and that a feeding trout can sense a fly letting behind it. It is also worth saying that, I am sure I would have taken that fish on a variety of small flies but only if they had landed in that one small spot. My wife forgave me for being late home but Melle, after sniffing around my clothes to get the story of the day, went off and sulked for a while.

These stories may give the impression that trout are on the move in August, but in some seasons the opposite is certainly the norm. Although the dead summer period varies from year to year, it can get into late August before the water comes to life again. The few fish that can be seen feeding though the first half of the month are often taking a small midge of one sort or other.

The midge family have become recognised as an important fly on still waters but are often ignored on rivers. Some species have a yearly life cycle while

c.Ashley Hunter

G. Ashley Hunter

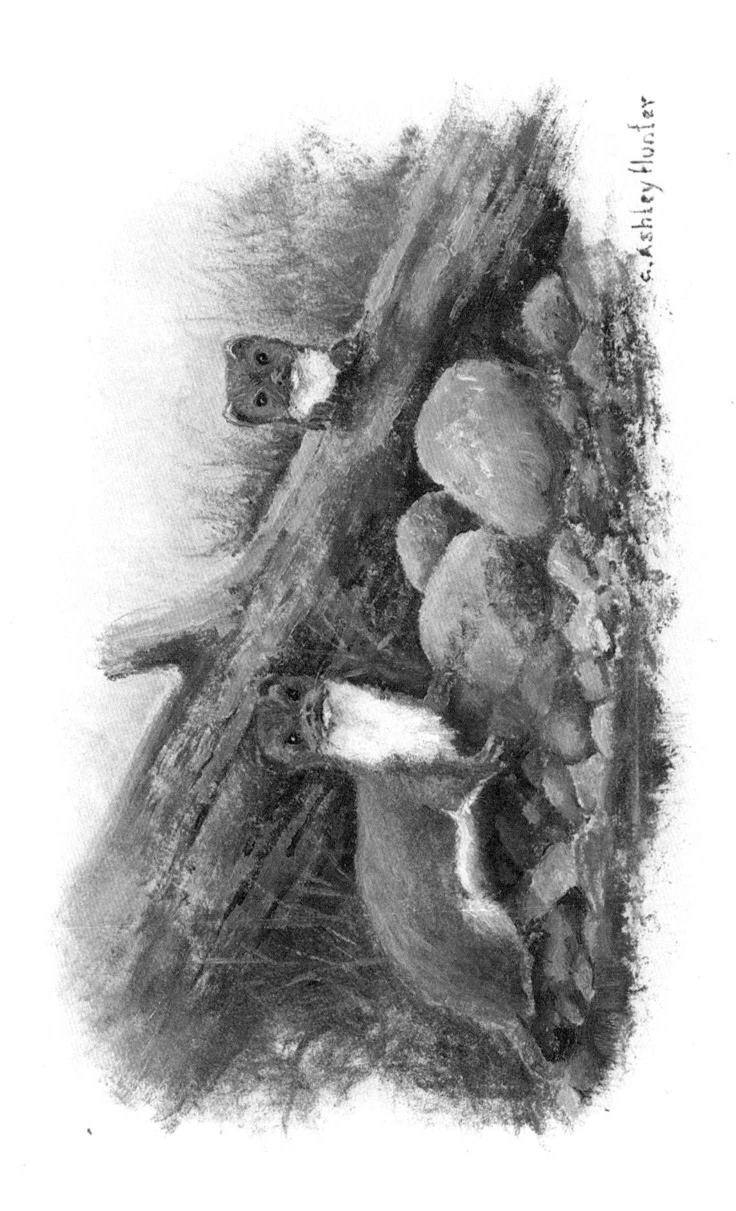

G.Ashley Hunter

others can produce as many as three generations in one season. They mostly have one thing in common, that as the mature pupae emerge, they swim slowly to the surface where the winged adult finally develops. During that last stage the pupae hang just beneath the surface film and it is then that trout take their fill. Having said this, I must add that there are often so few midge hatching on moving water that it is perhaps easier to pretend that you have not seen them.

Often the larger midge species hatch out either early or late in the day, so alas it is the smaller ones that hatch through the midday hours. I say 'alas' because my finger and eye functions struggle below hook size 14, and if one is to match these day-hatching midge, a size 16 or even 18 is needed.

To fish those small flies properly you have to use a lightweight leader of 2lbs or less. If you manage to tie your tiny size 18 fly on your fine leader you then find that the tender brookside grasses of spring have now become as tough as old boots. Every wispy grass leaf seems to have a breaking strain of 4lbs or more and by late August they all now lean a little further over the water.

There are so many midge patterns to choose from that I hesitate to make any recommendation. A traditional Blae and Black wet fly, fished just below the surface, is perhaps as good a general purpose to imitate the dying midge. Or try a dry fly to imitate the egg-laden female as she dips into the surface to lay her eggs. Better still, do as I do - if on a warm August afternoon when the trout are only taking midge - stretch out in the sunshine, close your eyes and dream about big fat mayfly. It will do you - and your temper - much more good.

The bird activity is always changing; by August the young have become stronger and more venturesome in flight. To prove it an early hatch of young mallards flew along the brook. One of the visiting herons had brought his offspring for a training session, and the young heron stood on the bank while dad, demonstrating the art of quiet stillness, stood in the brook. Both the heron parents seem to take responsibility for feeding and training their young, often separately like this. There was one occasion when I did manage to watch a family group round a pond. Four young herons were being guided and fed by both parents. One immature heron sat on the fence; two were on the bank and the other stood in the edge of the pond. But all were absolutely still, just watching their parents in the water's edge. I too sat absolutely still for most of an hour, watching them, and in that time the young moved no more than a foot. My children were young then - how I wished that I could have the same control over them.

Our kingfishers also become more active in August. Although I have never been able to watch them I know they do feed the young for a while after they leave the nest. At the same time I am sure they demonstrate to the young the best fishing techniques. By late August the parents, having truly had enough of family life, drive the young kingfishers away to find a length of water for themselves. What seems to be a hard and ruthless event, happily also creates a lot of kingfisher activity along the brook, with more sightings than usual. It is this time of year when kingfishers are more likely to raid your garden pond. To a young bird, driven away from home and forced to fend for himself, a garden pond full of tame goldfish must truly seem like Heaven.

The hot weather brings the dairy cow herd down into the water to cool off. As they stand around enjoying the coolness round their legs, the water gets churned and disturbed. I have tried fishing in the coloured water below the cows without success but on a few occasions I have taken trout from alongside dabbling mallard. The trout must have learned that dabbling ducks disturb juicy insects, flushing them out of the weeds. That herd of cows share both the brook and the low meadow with us. After early morning milking, although there is a perfectly good bridge, they prefer walking to the far meadows through the brook, returning again for a drink and a cool paddle in the afternoon.

At this time of year there are some newly

calved cows in the herd. The young calves are left back in the farm buildings whilst their mums are sent out with the herd to graze through the day. Unfortunately by early afternoon these cows, having had a good feed of grass, get restless for their calves. The gate is closed, and they know that they can't get out of the field, but they can keep having a look just in case - and all this takes place with a chorus of moos and a lot of splashing in and out of the brook.

8
SEPTEMBER

Where the cows cross back and forth, deep channels have formed in the bank sides with the constant tread of hooves. This is a natural ford which, before the bridge was built, would have been used by sheep and horses as well as cattle. This light, easily worked soil would be some of the first land farmed in the county, which means that this ford could have been a crossing for the farmer and his beasts for six thousand years or more. It is quite understandable that the banks have got a bit eroded in that time, resulting in a wide ford now stretching some forty metres along our open length. We only see the smallest trout in this shallow water.

"LOOK OUT FRED, ITS MILKING TIME AGAIN"

Most years we have to wait until early September to see a really good hatch of the most common of the crane-fly species, better known as daddy-long-legs. Before the mayfly came back in numbers, I called the daddy-long-legs the poor man's mayfly. Not that daddies hatch in water, nor does the brook play any part in their life cycle, but enough fall into the water by accident to include them in our year. In fact I could have included them in this story at any time from mid-July but those early season daddies are seldom numerous enough to excite the trout.

Daddies lay their eggs in the grass sward down in among the very base of the plants. Leather jackets is the distinctive name given to these hungry ugly grubs that hatch from the eggs and farmers hate them. They don't eat the whole foliage of a plant but just nibble through the plant stems at ground level, which of course kills the whole plant. Occasionally a bad infestation of leather jackets can bare the grass in ever enlarging circles of about ten or twelve feet across. I have turned over a few clods and stones on the outer ring of such a circle to find hundreds of grubs hiding through the daylight hours. Alas, even after ploughing in a turf, eggs that were previously laid in growing grass sward will still hatch out the following spring, when they eat whatever crop the unlucky farmer has sown there.

In my early teens I used them as bait for

coarse fishing but despite their tough sounding name the fish seemed to pinch them of the hook too often, without getting caught. In the days of hand picking potatoes the leather jackets were spun out with the early season potatoes. One day I picked up about fifteen and put them in an old tobacco tin. Unfortunately when it rained that night I forgot about them. Looking in the tin two or three days later, I found just two big fat leather jackets watching each other warily from opposite sides of the tin.

Many larvae are carnivorous; one of the most ferocious is the larva of the great diving beetle. When my children were young I brought in some frogspawn, put it in a goldfish bowl along with some pondweed for the young tadpoles to feed on. The children enjoyed watching them hatch but after a few days the tadpoles numbers seemed to be falling. At morning coffee time I pulled up a chair and watched. Hidden in the edge of the pondweed were two tiny larvae, hardly half an inch long. When a tadpole swam near to one it made a sudden pounce, gripping the tadpole with two curved spikes that looked like over sized top teeth. I presume it injected some form of acid into the tadpole to liquefy its inside, which it then sucked out. Anyway the dead empty tadpole shell sank to the bottom. It was fascinating to observe them for about a week or two, until there were only five or six tadpoles left. By then the larvae were a good inch long and growing fast. The children had to decide between our five future frogs or those two tigers of the pond.

This year, when the real hatch of daddies came in September, our brook had become very difficult to fish. There was so much weed debris in the water, a good thunder storm was badly needed to flush it out. Trout nose in amongst this bottom weed trash for the many insects hiding and feeding amongst it. To get to these bottom feeding trout some fishermen use a weighted shrimp on the point, with an easily seen dry fly on the first dropper as a bite indicator. That way they can fish in the deeper water but hopefully still see the gentle autumn take. Alas when I tried it, each cast collected its share of slimy weed to the extend that I found no pleasure in the method.

The benefit that these big fat daddies - the fat ones are the egg laden females - bring to our fishing, is simply that they make the trout look up with some expectation. Although fish have no idea when one will drop in - there can be two in five minutes or none for five hours - our trout take them all. I have caught trout on nicely tied daddies, by that I mean near perfect ones that lie life-like on the water with all legs intact. Once they have caught a fish or even been in and out of a fly box a few times they become mis-shaped, which can make them useless when trying to fool a wary trout.

I have two stories to illustrate this from a past

year, when again there was a good hatch of daddies on the meadows. I found the most presentable daddy in my box, straightened out its legs as best I could, and cast it upstream to a feeding trout. I have always had most success by just letting them float with the flow of water, and when this one came back towards me I could see a trout keeping station some six inches below the daddy, and with eyes glued on the fly, it sailed right past me - but it didn't take.

Later in the day I saw another fish follow a heavily bloated female daddy right across the brook. This time though, the real daddy was flying just a bit too high to tempt the trout to rise. Seeing where the fish came out from under the tips of the damsel grass, I changed to a grey-brown sized twelve hackled fly. He rose to it the first cast. As it came to the net I lost the trout in the edge of this intrusive damsel grass but that's a price worth paying to hold both wildlife and fish. The real point of the story is - that hatching daddies bring fish up to the surface to feed but you don't necessarily have to fish an artificial daddy to catch them. Likewise, although Bill claims no success with artificial daddies, he seems to have good sport with other flies when daddies are about in numbers.

There is always a danger from wasps, because they like to nest along any brook bank. Sliding down the bank one day to try a cast from a sitting position under an overhanging willow, as my line hit the water,

I realised there was a wasps' nest right by me. I was holding the rod right over the entrance. I managed to creep away without getting stung. A few days later the badgers had dug out that nest, and, immune to stings, they had eaten all the grubs, but there were still a lot of live wasps about. Without the nest to keep them warm at night, and a queen to lead them, those wasps would all die. Until then though the dopey wasps can be very angry and aggressive. Luckily I saw the danger and fished elsewhere.

Because my wife is very allergic to stings, whenever there are a lot of wasps around our home I bravely set out to find their nest. Several times, when I have had no success in my search, a few days later a

'THE STING IN THE TAIL'

badger has dug out a nest that I had walked past. Brock's nose is obviously better in the dark than my eyesight is in daylight.

September became a very sad month. I lost Melle. She had been my constant fishing and shooting companion for so many years, but the time had gone so quickly, when the vet asked me her age, I got it wrong by two years. The house seemed empty, both Celia and I were so lost without her. Although I still have my white cat to take for a walk, it does not have the same response, and like all cats, if it is not in the mood, you have to walk on your own.

The week after Melle died I had one free day to fish, when neither Bill nor Gerald were free to go. I found it hard to go on my own, knowing that without her I would not have the patience to fish a fly successfully. In the end I decided to fish the lower length under the alders where hopefully there would be some action without too much concentration. Digging in the hard dry ground only produced four worms, so I called in at the tackle shop for a few maggots. It was a case of anything to take my mind off my dog - I suppose I bought a few things that shouldn't be mentioned in a fly fishing book. Then to compound the sin, when I got to the brook the cows were splashing about where I had wanted to fish, and I ended up on our fly length.

There was a more serious purpose to my day.

A fishing club further up the brook had stocked their length with grayling about two years prior. We had each caught three or four by accident when we were fishing after trout and, as none of us had any experience of grayling, I thought that I would try one or two different baits to see if there was any response.

There weren't many daddies about, in fact there was not a trout moving anywhere. I decided to try a spell of standard down stream wet fly fishing in the best pool but with no luck. This is the pool where I have caught one or two nice roach, so in my restless state I decided to try for one. Floating a small fly down with two maggots attached, with the line always tight, soon became boring, so, for a change, I decided to try a worm, letting it float down with the flow of water. I got no result, but instead of moving along the brook with a wet fly, I just added more weight and cast the worm back in, thinking that I would just sit for a while and daydream.

Memories of Melle came to haunt me; her concentration when I was fishing and her disappointment when one got away. When I lost a fish she would often sit by that spot, just mournfully staring into the water. To put one back was in her view a terrible crime, she would watch that spot for several minutes. Occasionally if a returned trout rested in the shelter of the weeds along the edge of the brook (and if I was not looking) Melle would reach in, sometimes with head completely

under water, to gently lift it out again and bring it to me unmarked.

When all these memories got too much I decided to go up to the farm for a chat. Winding in the worm I felt a heart-skipping tug but it turned out to be just a small pike - but with that one on the bank the day was not all wasted. I also resolved to learn more about the beautiful grayling species and how or when to fish for it.

I have never been without a dog. A journalist once wrote an article about me, which started with these words, “He runs his farm with his two dogs and his wife Celia.” Well you can imagine that “his wife Celia” didn’t fully appreciate the order of merit.

When my son took over our farm, my collie dog stayed with him, but of course Melle came with us to the bungalow. After about a week of mourning for Melle, Celia put the 'dogs for sale page' from the local paper in front of me, then suggested that it was time to, "do something." All our married life we have had either one or two black labradors, so we were not going to change breed now.

Even with the breed decision made, choosing the right pup is still not easy. We go for a homebred pup where both parents are working dogs and also family companions. We would only buy a kennel-bred pup if we were sure that its parents had a close, everyday companionship with their owner. Genetics play a major part in dog behaviour, and a breeder selects his breeding for the trait he wants, but if we want a dog that bonds well, it then makes sense to select our pup from parents that have done just that.

After several phone calls we went to look at a litter owned by a young keeper. The bitch was his personal dog and shared his home and his life. We arrived in his yard just as the keeper returned from feeding his pheasants. The pup's mother sat proudly by his side in the front of the Landrover. She looked a happy, good-humoured dog; the last thing we wanted was to end up with a sulky dog. The sire was owned by a member of his shoot and again enjoyed the same relationship with his owner. The fact that neither had a field trial champion in their close pedigree did not bother us.

With seven identical bitch pups to select from it was an interesting experience. When we thought we had spotted one that we liked it would get lost in the next rough and tumble. One returned to Celia a few times (well we thought it was the same one) so she picked it up and we had our pup. We parked down the small lane and over a cup of coffee chose the name Becky. She has proved to be one of the most responsive and easily trained dogs we have ever owned.

When the badly needed thunder finally came to flush out the brook, of course it left high and deeply coloured water. It was such a relief to cast a fly without collecting weed that I spent a happy two hours just doing that but without a touch or sight of a fish. Later in the day although the water was falling it was still far from clear; in fact I suspected that someone was doing earth work of some kind higher up the brook, it was so discoloured.

As there was nothing to see in the dirty water I moved down stream among the trees. I soon found that a few fish were feeding deep down in the holes among the alder roots, which made fishing quite difficult. Because these bottom feeding fish are usually the larger older trout, some of which feed exclusively on snails, it is no harm to take a few this close to the end of the season. Alas it is far from easy to present a fly properly to trout lying in the deep holes amongst the many alder roots.

My September story seems a little disappointing for a fly fishing record, especially because it can be a very pleasant fly-fishing month. In past years, once there had been some late summer rain to wash out the brook, and with a reasonable water level fish could be on the move throughout the day. Trout that are difficult to catch in August become less selective in September and - fished with caution and care - can give a lot of pleasure.

A couple of years back, when Gerald was having a course of chemotherapy, we went down to the brook on a mild September day. Although a few fish were moving we had to wander to find them. We met later in the afternoon just below the bridge. Gerald had caught a nice brace and was telling me about them over a flask of coffee when another fish rose just below the bridge. Because we only have access to one bank, from the bridge down, and because a clump of alders prevented casting up to it from our bank, the only way to cover that trout was to float a fly down under the bridge. So when Gerald set out to net his third fish of the day, he had to climb down a near vertical ten foot bank, that would have challenged a goat, then balance precariously at the bottom to cast.

I had to wait a while but eventually the fly came floating from under the bridge, right on the spot, with the leader and fly in line to prevent drag - and Gerald caught his third trout. I have never discussed bending a fly line with either Gerald or Bill (I am afraid that they might ask for a demonstration) but there was no way that Gerald could cover that trout without casting across and bending his leader down with the current. It probably took him ten minutes to get in the right position to make that one cast - but one was enough. It illustrates the difference between fishing a small river as against a stocked pond. There you can cast away for half an hour between fish. Here you can spend that half hour finding and plotting how to get just one cast into just one fish.

I have watched both Gerald and Bill, casting left handed, curling their cast around trees and swinging it in under branches to land in spots that I with a right hand cast can only envy. I have never really mastered the art of backhand casting, or to put it more clearly, casting over my left shoulder with my right hand. Although I do sometimes cast that way, and even take some fish, I am untidy and scare a lot more than I should. There is no doubt that to get satisfaction out of a small river, such as ours, it pays to improve your skill with a short rod. The ability to cast over either shoulder enables you to cover more fish, perhaps one feeding behind a tree, and otherwise out of reach.

The other skill, that I have not mentioned, is a roll cast, which is casting your line out again without a back cast. If you wish to stand in the brook under the low branches it's a must. Again it's a skill that I am not good at. Although I manage to roll out a wet fly, alas, I don't seem to have the lightness of touch to fish a dry fly that way.

9
OCTOBER

Blood in the Dew

Life anew as the sun awakes from slumber,
Beaming and smiling over distant hillstops,
To shimmer and glisten on dew sodden pastures.
Where bovine feet splashing home for milking,
Create dark green trails through the finest of webs.
Millions of spiders, cursing cloven hooves passage,
Scurry to repair their designs for death's harvest.
Then before the moon can fade into its heaven,
Hundreds of starlings in need of a breakfast,
Descend to devour great hordes of the spiders,
Engrossed in the bounty, yet arguing at morsels.
The hawk is among them before they get airborne,
The squawks tell of pain - black feathers say death.
Two carrion crows see it as one free for taking.
As the hawk defends with rapier sharp talons,
Cawing beaks' stab with deadly precision,
None see the buzzard soaring high over treetops.
His stoop is spectacular and this time on target.

If the sun rising higher is a herald to living,
Then blood in the dew says all life has a price

Through late September and October trout can again often be feeding on what drops in from above. Although I have seen a few olives hatching on a warm early October afternoon that was an exception, but trout can still be feeding high in the water if it is reasonable clear.

The early morning October sun reveals a carpet of spiders' webs across the meadow. A fantastic sight created by millions of spiders. In fact the money-spider population alone can be one and a half million to each acre. No I didn't count them - I read it in a book. Along the open lengths of a brook such as this, where grass leaning over the water's edge provides the main shelter for fish, spiders must drop into the water in considerable numbers. Birds and other insects also feast on the young spiders, so in most species mum spider allows for this mass slaughter by laying hundreds of eggs. A garden spider is known to lay up to 800 eggs in each of two clutches.

The early morning sun will also show single strands of web strung from bush to bush like super fine Christmas decorations. When I was young I used to wonder how they did it, how did a spider cross a three metre gap from one tree to the next? Time revealed the answer for me. Some species of money-spiders anchor themselves with a single strand of web and launch out into the breeze to paraglide to the next bush or tree branch.

A few years ago I went to judge the stick dressing competition at a ploughing match in early October. The Secretary entertained me to a free lunch in the refreshment tent before the work commenced. All through the meal money-spiders were landing on my salad. We were sitting about a 100 yards from the nearest tree so those spiders must also have the ability to release that anchor and float through the air using that long single strand of web to keep them airborne in the breeze. Later, in the stick tent, the steward had to wipe a spider off nearly every stick before passing them to me. As an aside there were over 160 sticks to handle, examine, compare and place in order of merit. With some twenty or more proud stickmakers watching my every move, I dare not miss looking at even the crudest (not that there were many) of sticks. By the time I had finished, I was completely 'knackered'!

When those young spiders are on the move in the autumn many end up in the brook. Grayling fishermen seem to rate the spider higher than any other autumn fly. They favour a size sixteen or even eighteen but I splash about with a size fourteen. There are many imitation spider flies to choose from, if you have not got one just fish an olive or a greenwell.

Rain and thunder is often a feature of autumn, this year was no exception with heavy thunderstorms early in the month raising the water into a racing torrent. After a few days of fine weather I thought it might be worth a visit but when I saw how high the brook was running I had no desire to cast a fly.

Although I have included fishing with worms on occasions to try to show that we are not fishing snobs (many fly fishermen are), I realise now that the worming stories in this book are completely out of proportion. This season I have only fished a worm three times and told you about all of them. And in fact I only tied a wet fly on about four or five times, whereas there has been numerous enjoyable days with a dry fly that I have not included. My real pleasure comes from casting a dry fly. Well, it is more than just casting, it is the skill and experience needed to achieve the downfall of a particular fish, and a dry fly is the most exiting way to achieve it.

Seeing a trout rise, perhaps in a difficult spot that needs a bit of thought and planning before you can even get a fly over it, then actually getting into the right position with the right fly, can all take some time. The final thrust of the bullfighter's sword kills the bull, but the real skill of the matador is in his finesse of movement with cape and feet, well before then. With a fly rod the end can be just one cast for one trout, but the satisfaction is in the whole experience leading up to that cast. As those who fish will know, it is not that simple. Many times I fail along the way, either in the planning or the execution, but the worst failure is when I do everything right only to spoil it all by a bad cast at the end.

I have noticed through the years that all three of us have times when the sheer pleasure of casting a fly takes president over the canny skill of catching a trout. Yes the two are different on any water but particularly in a small river or brook. Those who would aspire to this type of fishing must learn their field craft to be successful. There are times when the fish are not moving and you have to work hard. Then, of course, the more casts you make, the more water you cover, the more chance there is of a fish.

Our host farmer does not fish but his wife does; despite offers of fly tuition she still fishes a worm but with great skill. They are both keen gardeners and any worm dug up is kept in a bucket of old clods for future use. On a nice afternoon, with a few worms and the dog for company, she enjoys her walk along their brook. Traditional Cheshire farmers have their dinner at midday, which of course is their main meal. In the evening they have tea, which is a lighter meal. On the afternoons that his wife has fished, this lucky man comes into tea to find a large trout, cooked with butter and almonds, all wrapped up in tinfoil, just ready to slide onto his plate. Now you know why he will not allow a fly fishing only rule.

Can I claim that my fly fishing is somehow more enjoyable then than her humble worm; nonsense. Each method can give equal pleasure to different people. One October, a couple of years back, I got down to the brook side just after lunch, intending to fish through until evening. For the time of year it was a warm pleasant day and there was even one or two fish rising. I enjoyed stalking them. I even hooked two, one on a greenwell and the other on a spidery looking nymph, but they were only lightly hooked so I lost both. Whilst I was fishing I was greeted by the farm dog and turned to receive a wave from his mistress as she went to fish the lower length of brook.

I am not pretending that I fished solidly until

night; by mid afternoon the warm sun and the dry grass tempted both me and the dog to stretch out. We woke refreshed to try again but still failed to take a fish. Breaking off for a cup of Earl Grey and my share of a sandwich, I was surprised when a cold wind got up as the sun went lower. It ended what had been a very pleasant if blank late summer day.

Calling in at the farmhouse for a chat, the lovely aroma of trout cooked in butter and almonds met me. Whilst I had fished for some six hours, give or take the odd sleep, this accomplished woman had caught two large trout (she usually catches larger fish than we do on fly), cleaned and cooked them. Having both dined on one fish, the other trout was kept to eat cold with a salad the next day. Alas I arrived at the washing up stage with the delicious smells still lingering in the air. I had enjoyed my day but I had to admit that - at that moment - it was me who felt more than a tinge of envy. There is no way I am going to tell her that if she has not fished with a fly she has not fished, what snobbish nonsense. But fly-fishing is addictive and can take a hold of you to an extent that other methods cease to give such pleasure.

Bill has reached that stage, and keeps a firm hold of his fly rod. When he fishes the lower length he usually gets down into the water to cast under the tree canopy with a wet fly. Whereas late in the season, Gerald will still take a worm and have an enjoyable hour under the dense alder trees.

There is no doubt that late summer trout are

harder to catch; it is not just because of what they are eating. The metabolism of the trout changes as the summer progresses. Spring fish are desperate to feed, whilst winter fish feed very little, and in between, in late summer, trout become lethargic and dilatory. When I was suffering from that trapped nerve in my neck, a couple of seasons ago, moving about with a fly rod was difficult. I tended to sit in one place and wait for a fish to get hungry. One day I passed the time by dropping the wet fly in the water up stream from me so that it floated down, opposite to where I lay hidden on the bank. With my lower face masked by the grass and my hat pulled down to my sunglasses I could see the fly in the clear water. Two different trout took it and released it, each time so gently that neither was detectable with the rod. I have no doubt that in spring both would have taken that fly with a knock hard enough to have hooked themselves.

Even when the high water subsided this October I had difficulties making time to fish before the season ended, so I have including a few stories from the past. One of the strangest was in the stomach contents of a one and a half pound trout. I have not lost the habit of checking each fish I clean, and in this one there was a bat, only a small bat, but how did that trout take it? I don't think it was a pipistrelle, which with a body only the length of a matchstick is the most common and smallest of our bats. I have little knowledge of bats but after a visit to the library I believe that it was a Daubenton's, which are very slightly larger than the pipistrelle.

Still with the library's extensive textbook, it told me that it is the Daubentons that we fishermen see most often at night as they skim across the water taking flies and insects in the late dusk. I suppose it must be inevitable that the odd young bat will have an accident whilst he learns the art of taking his supper from just above the wave tops.

There is one of Britain's largest bats along this brook -the largest is the noctule or great bat. The one we occasionally see here is the serotine, which is only slightly smaller, but its long shaggy blackish coat and broad wings make it look very large. Quartering the ground looking for insects, with a wingspan of about one foot, their heavily laboured flight can be startling in the late dusk. Although I understand they are fairly common in the South East, they are seldom seen in this area. My only sightings have been very late in the evening, by the brook, and along the lane on my journey home.

The banks on the lower length rise straight up from the water for about three to four feet. On this lower length between the many trees our bank is fairly clear of weeds, whilst, with the stock fence standing on the other side, that bank gets overgrown with bushes and tall weeds. On one occasion, Bill was in the water trying to float a wet fly round a corner created by the alder tree trunks, when there was a disturbance among the nettles on the far bank. He looked up as a rabbit leapt into the brook within feet of him. Then a fox skirted the bogs of nettles on the bank in an attempt to intercept its victim, and the rabbit, jumping through the shallow water along the edge, splashed past Bill in its desperation to escape the fox.

Bill watched expectantly, just as I came blundering up and of course both fox and rabbit vanished. Bill was not pleased with me, in fact I think it's the only time in the years we have been friends that I have heard a hint of anger in his voice.

Before the bats hibernated, and the trout fishing season ended, I was determined to get down to the brook one last time. It was time to introduce Becky, my three months old Labrador pup, to my hobby. She had not been in the car since we bought her and obviously she did not reckon much to it. In fact I had to chase after her before I could get her into it. As soon as we got to the brook, I decided to have an early lunch to show the pup that fishing had its good points. A few well-placed crusts soon had her jumping in and out of the car with confidence. Like all Labradors, Becky loved the excitement of the water but alas I could not show her a fish this day.

The dams had not been removed before the heavy September rain raised the water levels, and it was now the end of the season. At last the water had fallen enough to try - even then it was a precarious job, so I was grateful for the skilled help of my nephew. He, with a volunteer helper, donned their waders, to stand in the full force of water, passing stones one to another. They had arrived whilst I was fishing, and with the pup skipping around, I watched the two strong young men struggle to balance against the power of a brook still invigorated by the autumn rain. There were some dangerous moments, and four wet sleeves, before all the rocks were piled on the bank.

It was a fitting last day of an enjoyable season. I hope you have enjoyed sharing it with us. With a new dog to help with both my fishing, and my butties, next season beckons anew. With it would come more experiences for the three of us on this lovely little river in the heart of Cheshire - and for Bill to capture on canvas for all to enjoy.

The trees stand naked in the breeze,
The flies have seen their summer.
Yet can there be just one last tug
To tip the heart to its flutter phase?

Or is that the season over?

It seems that only weeks have gone,
Since turning seventy young fish out.
And was it all those years ago,
I first stalked a cunning trout?

Can it be I am getting older?

The banksides are getting steeper
Hook eyes are getting smaller.
The mud seems to be more sticky
And the car park's got further.

I wonder, are my seasons over?

On stark branches bare and brown
Swell the buds for future glory.
And in that water dark and cold
Larvae wait to relive the story.

Ah yes, my grandson wants a rod.